G000016691

Memories of

Milton Keynes

Memories of
Milton Keynes

Marion Hill

TEMPUS

Frontispiece: Young Kevin Parker, Netherfield Cubs pack member, gets the feel of the job of holding the balloons, April 1982, in preparation for the famous 'Red Balloon' advertisement for Milton Keynes, released throughout the nation that year.

First published 2005

Tempus Publishing Limited
The Mill, Brimscombe Port,
Stroud, Gloucestershire, GL5 2QG

© Marion Hill, 2005

The right of Marion Hill to be identified as the Author
of this work has been asserted in accordance with the
Copyrights, Designs and Patents Act 1988.

All rights reserved. No part of this book may be reprinted
or reproduced or utilised in any form or by any electronic,
mechanical or other means, now known or hereafter invented,
including photocopying and recording, or in any information
storage or retrieval system, without the permission in writing
from the Publishers.

British Library Cataloguing in Publication Data.
A catalogue record for this book is available from the British Library.

ISBN 0 7524 3397 0

Typesetting and origination by Tempus Publishing Limited
Printed in Great Britain

Contents

Introduction 6

Acknowledgements 6

Sources 7

one Homes and Families 9

two Schooldays and Training 21

three Working Life 33

four Entertainment and Leisure 45

five Wartime and Hard Times 59

six New City Development 69

seven Country Folk and City Slickers 83

eight Communities and Friends 95

nine Unforgettable Moments,
Memorable People 107

ten Changing Worlds 117

Introduction

People living in the Milton Keynes area forty years ago came under the auspices of three towns, thirteen villages and a county council. There have only been two agencies whose sole responsibility has been Milton Keynes: the Milton Keynes Development Corporation (MKDC), the Government-sponsored organization whose remit from 1967 until 1992 was to build the new city; and Milton Keynes Council, which currently oversees the services for more than 200,000 people.

Now, on the eve of further proposed expansion, this book is offered as a testament to, and a celebration of, the unique character of the city and is dedicated to the citizens of Milton Keynes who have invested their energies and their futures in this remarkable – and enduring – venture.

Marion Hill

Acknowledgements

All contributions come from the vast oral archive kept at the Living Archive of Milton Keynes, many from its recent Heritage Lottery Fund project, The People's History of Milton Keynes. A registered charity, the Living Archive has been collecting reminiscences from city residents since 1975 – thousands of hours of taped interviews – belying the claim that purpose-built new communities 'have no history'. Its documentary and photographic archive of the city area and of erstwhile rural and small town communities, is a unique and precious historical resource to which I am very grateful to have enjoyed free and helpful access. Its bedrock is that 'everyone has a story to tell' – a stunningly simple and powerful definition of history. It should be unstintingly supported so that new generations of the city can contribute their stories of life in the Milton Keynes community of the twenty-first century.

Living Archive (LA) is based at The Old Bath House, 212 Stratford Road, Wolverton, MK12 5RL, 01908 322568; (see also www.livingarchive.org.uk). Many thanks too for access to the archives of English Partnerships, Milton Keynes Parks Trust and Bletchley Park Trust, (01908 640404 and www.bletchleypark.org.uk). Essential reading for anyone researching the development of the new city is *Milton Keynes, Image and Reality* by Terence Bendixson and John Platt, Granta, 1992.

Sources

Interview transcripts, letters, diaries, newspapers and logs produced by people living in Milton Keynes city area from 1860 and collected since 1975 by the Living Archive:

Elizabeth Ainge, Wolverton
Mustafa A. Alami, Greenleys
Malcolm Anderson, Woughton-on-the-Green
Dicky Arnold, Bletchley
Philip Ashbourn, Great Linford
Monica Austin, Bletchley
Kathy Baker, Great Linford
Brian Barnes, Stony Stratford
Samantha Bassnett, North Furzton
Meg Bates, Fenny Stratford
Ken Beeley, Bletchley
Soraya Billimoria, Downs Barn
Frank Bodimead, Bletchley
David Bodley, Loughton
Reginald Booth, Castlethorpe
Eileen Bowen, Bletchley
Peter Bowtell, Calverton
Annie Bradstock, New Bradwell
Bucks Advertiser and Aylesbury News
Peter Bunnage, Shenley Church End
Sue Burrows, Great Linford
Kathy Chapman, Furzton
Wai Kau Chan, Milton Keynes
George Chandler, Old Bletchley
Helen Cheuk, Furzton
Guiseppe Ciliberti, Bletchley
Leroy Clarke, Beanhill
Betty Clifford, Bletchley
Geoff Cooksey, Great Linford
Eileen Cordon, Bletchley
Arthur Cowley, Stony Stratford
Henry Dewick, Wolverton
Donato Distazio, Emerson Valley
May Dunmille, Wolverton

Rosemary Evans, Bletchley
Jeff Fawcett, Newport Pagnell
Ravi Fernandez, Willen
Adelaide Fielding, Stantonbury
Ivy Fisher, Old Bletchley
Ronald Flinn, Bletchley and Wolverton
Stephen Flinn, Stony Stratford
Zena Flinn, Stony Stratford
Marion Fox, Wavendon Gate
Clarence Vincent Gill, Wolverton
Debbie Greaves, Stony Stratford
Arthur Grigg, Bletchley
Bernard Groom, Shenley Brook End
A Guide to Wolverton Works
Neil Higson, Cosgrove
Bob Hill, Ravenstone
Harry J. Hippsley, Wolverton
Margaret Hiscock, Wolverton
Norma Jamieson, Woughton Park
Mick Kelly, Greenleys
Tony King, Woughton
Lawrence (Lol) King, Woughton
Roger Kitchen, Wolverton
Amy Knill, Old Bletchley
Mabel Kong, Stantonbury
Audrey Lambert, Stony Stratford
Richard Leung, Oldbrook
Chun Yau Leung, Bolbeck Park
Arthur Lewis Lloyd, Wolverton
Carole Loxton, Woughton Park
Norma Loh, Neath Hill
Sue Malleson, Bow Brickhill
Rodney Markley, Great Linford
Alan Marshall, Bletchley

Gordon Marshall, Bletchley
Wendy Marshall, Bletchley
Roy Maycock, Bletchley
Brenda Monaghan, Bletchley
Lesley Moore, Wolverton
Hawtin Mundy, New Bradwell
John Napleton, Simpson Village
Pat Old, Great Holm
Brian O'Sullivan, New Bradwell
Kenneth Page, Castlethorpe
Sandra Page, Castlethorpe
Cecil Palmer, Stony Stratford
Pushpa Pandit, Stantonbury
C.A. Park, Wolverton
Ron Perry, Bradwell Village
Donato Piselli, Wolverton
Ernest Pye, Tinkers Bridge
Gordon Ridgeway, Bletchley
Neville Rose, Bletchley
Francesco Russo, Bletchley
'NS', Stony Stratford
Brian Salter, Newport Pagnell
Ruth Salter, Newport Pagnell
Kathy Sellick, Heelands
Ratilal Hirji Shah, Milton Keynes
June Shrewsbury, New Bradwell
Pam Sinfield, Woughton-on-the-Green
Trevor (Sam) Sinfield, Woughton-on-the-Green
K. Skinner, Wolverton
William Slee, Bletchley

Ernie and Muriel Smith, Stony Stratford
David Stabler, Neath Hill
J. Stallard, Wolverton
Ron Staniford, Bletchley
John Staniland, Pennylands
George Stephenson, Old Bradwell
Jack Stephenson, Bradville
Eliana Stovold, Great Linford
Tina Strutton, New Bradwell
Maralyn Tamblin, Milton Keynes
A. Tiffin, Stony Stratford
Ranjeet Toprani, Wolverton
Joan Thompson, Stantonbury
Peter Truscott, Shenley Brook End
Wayland Tunley, Woolstone
Janice Walker, Great Holm
Tracy Walters, New Bradwell
David Webb, Stony Stratford
Harry Welch, Wolverton
June Whittaker, Walnut Tree
Amy Williams, Stantonbury
Joseph Willis, Old Bradwell
Wolverton Express
Kwan Ying Wong, Bradwell Common
Mr Wong, Shenley Lodge
Samuel Wong, Blakelands
Tim Wong, Woolstone
F.G. Wood, Stantonbury
Peggy Yee, Conniburrow
Connie Yuen, Willen

Transcripts from Bletchley Park wartime employees 1939-1945, (courtesy of Bletchley Park Trust):

Marie Bennett
Marjorie Chapman
Rozanne Colchester
Mavis Faunch
Olive E. Keppel-Powis
Sheila Lancaster
Pamela O'Donahue

Winifred Ottery
Hilary Powell
Ruth Roberts
Anne Ross
Ruth Ross
Joyce Rushworth
G.E. Sweetland

one

Homes and Families

Summer House in the gardens of Wroughton Rectory, late nineteenth century.

Cottages that stood opposite the Swan Inn, Woughton-on-the-Green in the late 1880s and were demolished a few years later. From left to right: Martha Biggs (b.1820), Elsie Lee, Mary Biggs.

My father's house

When my father moved to York Road, Stony Stratford in 1910, the rent was 5s 6d a week. In 1918, they gave the tenants the option of buying. Each house was offered for sale at £225 – four bedrooms, front room, living room, kitchen, toilet outside and a barn to take two tons of coal. The highest price taken was £380 on the market.

Cecil Palmer

My mother-in-law's house

My mother-in-law came to Home Farm, Bletchley, after her marriage in 1886. When she died at ninety-three, the house was exactly as she had entered it: the beam across the kitchen ceiling with hooks for the side of bacon; the stone sink beside the copper in the corner; the vast black range with its open fire and side boiler for hot water; the second staircase leading to the bedroom overhead; a door leading along a corridor to the other bedroom, connected by the main staircase straight from the front door. The dairy still had lead troughs for salting the pig and churns for making butter.

Ivy Fisher

The house where I was born

I was born on Woodbine Terrace – a row of about ten small houses – in Bletchley in 1923. It's not there now. It was where the telephone exchange is at the corner of Church Street and Victoria Road. You went across the yard to the toilet and wash house. On the front you crossed the path to a little garden. Down the side was a small shop. On the other side was the garden of the Three Tuns pub, set on Watling Street.

Eileen Cordon

The stable was next door

We lived in at Stacey Hill Farm. My Dad had a wardrobe in the long bedroom, and an ottoman and table with a washing basin and the jug in it in the other bedroom. I slept there with me Mum and Dad. My sister, eight years older than me, had the long bedroom after she got married. I slept with me Dad after me Mum died. We used to do the cooking on the old fire and, later, two paraffin burners in the scullery. We had one big grandfather chair, a couch beside the window and a Welsh dresser put into the wall, where you put the crockery. The pantry jutted out into the bedroom and had a tiny window. There was a little wooden window in the bedroom looking into the stable, so if anything was wrong with the horses you could hear them and go out to them. During the war, a pony in there got its foot caught up in the manger. We stepped outside the door and the Home Guard challenged us. Of course you had to go through the rigmarole, didn't you – tell them if you were the enemy or foe and cor we didn't half swear at 'em and they came and helped us get the pony out.

Joseph Willis

My great-aunts

A great-aunt of mine in Clarence Road, Stony Stratford, was afraid of electricity. When she died, aged over ninety in the sixties, she still had gaslight. You used to pull the wire to light it. In the 1939–45 war, I had several holidays with a great-aunt in Shenley who lived in the almshouses. There was a double-fronted row of 'barns' in the gardens, one for each of the six houses – with a wooden-seated toilet. Newspaper was cut up and hung up on a string for toilet paper.

Audrey Lambert

Emptying the bucket

When we moved into our cottage in Bradwell village in 1946, the water tap was outside. We didn't have a flush toilet and there was no sewer. The council came round and emptied the buckets.

Ron Perry

Mother was the boss

Mother was the boss of the house, did all the washing. We had an old-fashioned copper with a fire underneath, a big iron mangle, and she did the washing for the whole of us on Monday. Tuesday ironing, Wednesday shopping. She used to shop [in Stony Stratford] at the Co-op and at Valentine the butcher. They killed their own meat in those days. Mum did all the work in the house. We children were expected to get out and play – we used to go off down the fields!

Cecil Palmer

A hard life

Mother had a hard life, boiling the coppers up in the barn to do the washing, cooking on the range – sometimes it would get hot and not cook well. On Sundays we would have relatives come all day, from Bletchley – she'd have to cook for them as well. She was a Bletchley girl from a building family. She hated it when she first came here [Woughton].

Tony King

Wives did not work

Wives did not work. Their job was to stay at home, keep it clean and tidy, look after the children and make sure there was a cooked meal on the table when the husband got home from work. There was no such things as microwaves and washing machines. If you

House in St James, Stony Stratford. From left to right: Father's mother, Ernest, Father, Mother with Stanley, Mother's mother, William, the maid. (courtesy of Dorothy Meadows)

were lucky, you had a Goblin vacuum cleaner. All the meals were cooked with fresh vegetables and the pies were home-made.

Ron Perry

Easter

Mum would always go back to Italian food, especially at Easter. She'd spend a lot of time making Easter bread and all the other Italian food. I can see her now, sitting on a chair with this big bowl. You could hear the plop-plop noise while she was making the dough. She'd put the container in the cupboard covered with blankets, and if they did not rise she'd put more yeast in them and start all over again. Shame, because nobody ate those cakes in the first place.

Eliana Stovold

Be quiet and eat up your tea

After school, we always listened to Children's Hour, with Uncle Mac and Larry the Lamb. The radio was a huge box about eighteen inches high and one foot deep with a knob on the side. When our programme finished, it was the Six O'Clock News when we did not have to talk. Father listened to the news. We'd be told, 'Be quiet and eat up your tea'. Tea would be bread and butter and cake. At Christmas, we hung up black woollen stockings over the brass knob at the head of the bed. This was filled during the night with oranges, nuts, chocolate, drawing books, pencils. Mother was Father Christmas – she put large presents in a pillowcase at the foot of the bed. The tree was planted back in the garden until the next year.

Audrey Lambert

Father prepared the vegetables

Our clothes were bought in Wolverton at Sharp's. Father would take two of us up on a Saturday afternoon and he would buy suits for us. The next week he'd take the other two. We had to make the suits last as long as we could. They were worn out when we'd done with them. Father used to wash and prepare the vegetables and do the garden. He had a workshop upstairs in the small bedroom and made no end of articles – tables, chairs and so on – all for the home.

Cecil Palmer

Sedate and irksome Sundays

My grandmother used to relate how the Rector [of St Mary's Church, Bletchley, c. 1900] expected everyone to attend service at least once every Sunday. If any member of his flock failed to do so, he would be sure to visit them during the week. Woe betide if no valid reason was forthcoming. There was no backsliding in his day. He was able to keep a paternal eye upon his children because Bletchley was a small village of about 100 houses until the First World War. Sunday was a day of rest and worship, no work. We went for long walks, most sedately, along the country lanes. No games could be played and this was most irksome.

Ivy Fisher

When my grandfather died

When my grandfather died, I remember being in one of the cars following the hearse, and when we passed the seat of elderly gentlemen outside the Plough Inn in Stony, they all stood up, took off their caps and bowed their heads. It was also the custom to draw all the curtains between the house of the deceased and the end of the road in which the hearse was to travel.

Audrey Lambert

Children playing in Silver Street, Stony Stratford, 1900.

We had a little cane

Our girls were brought up to be Church girls, same as we were. We were brought up properly and our two were. We had a little cane, just to whip the knuckles. We had it on the table every meal time, and if they didn't behave, you just had to pick it up. You never hit them, it was just a threat. If they put their elbows on the table they were told to take them off. You had to say 'Yes Sir' or 'Thank you Ma'am', and if you met ladies out you raised your hat, but you don't see that today. Of course, they don't wear hats today. We were told if we met an older person to always give way to them. There was no traffic then and we had to get into the road to let them pass on the pavement. We all had to do that.

Cecil Palmer

Home by ten

At home was strict. If we went out, we had to be home by ten. No kissing boys. My mum used to say we must not kiss boys otherwise we would get cold sores and things like that.

Eliana Stovold

A bit expensive

'My Dear Gladys,

How happy you have made me by your loving disposition and affectionate ways. I have absolutely made up my mind that I will always be true to you. Time will roll swiftly by when we shall always be together forever.' So wrote Leonard Kempster, twenty-four, a coach finisher at Wolverton, to Gladys Matilda Sykes, a single young woman who believed what her young man had written. As, however, he is earning £2 12s a week and preferred to remain in single blessedness, he was ordered by the Bench at Stony Stratford to pay 5s per week towards the upkeep of his child until the age of fourteen years. He had already settled his breach of promise with £35 down, so his letter and promise have been a bit expensive.

The *Bucks Advertiser and Aylesbury News*,
25 November 1916

The one for me

When my wife died, we had been married for fifty-five years. I was sixteen when we first met. I first saw her walking along the road and I said to myself 'She is the one for me'. And she was.

Ron Perry

We understood each other

I have been married for forty-one years. I did not speak much English when I met my wife, but we understood each other!

Francesco Russo

I didn't accept the marriage

My wife is my best companion because we have been married for thirty-seven years. We have known each other very well. All our children grew up here. They were educated by the local western culture. In the past I didn't accept interracial marriage because the marriage of a couple is not only their own business but also both families become relatives as well. Two years ago, my son wanted to get married with a local Welsh girl. At first I didn't accept the marriage, but they were so assertive and persistent that I had no choice. I made the concession. Nowadays, I'm totally changed. Obviously my daughter-in-law is not only very nice and well-educated, but also very much respects me as well. I feel very satisfied.

Tim Wong

Church Street, Wolverton, 1920s.

We compromise with each other

My son has married a white girl. He was seeing this girl behind my back. I said 'Bring the girl here. If I like her, you have Indian wedding, I'll accept the girl as my daughter-in-law. She'll be one of our family'. He brought the girl home and we talked and I think the girl is all right. Then he asked to bring her parents. The first thing the parents said, they wouldn't like their daughter to be converted. I said, 'We Hindus don't convert anyone. It is the Christian people or Muslims who convert'. I said openly, 'If she respects our religion, it's all right. If she doesn't, then it's no force'. And the girl has taken me, my family very well. She is getting fond of vegetarian food and she is very interested in Indian culture, Indian way of life, and, luckily, we compromise with each other.

Pushpa Pandit

Coming across the colour bar

I met my wife Eva in Wolverton. Her family goes back generations in Wolverton. Her grandfather was an undertaker, the Gurney's Undertakers. Her aunt also had a shop, a furniture removals firm. I remember going to a dance at McCorquodales where I worked and studied accountancy in the fifties. I went with Eva and a colleague and his girlfriend. We changed partners during the dance and she said to me, in ignorance, 'Do you ever come across the colour bar?' I said, 'Not until just now'.

Clarence Vincent Gill

Jolly good on the land

I married a Land Girl in the Second World War. At Bletchley, there was a place for Land Girls and they used to bring perhaps half a dozen out if you wanted them – when you were threshing, haymaking or harvesting. We were all quite pleased with them. My wife, she's dead now of course, she was excellent. She could in no time at all hand-milk and lamb a sheep or cow. She'd never done anything like that before. Came from Leicester actually. She was jolly good on the land. She came to work for us permanent. She lived in Simpson in lodgings.

Lol King

Farming Families

They do leave property around, farming families do.

Sam Sinfield

Extended families

Initially a lot of people were unhappy. They felt isolated – it wasn't the land of milk and honey after all. They came from extended families, very young people who hadn't learned the skills of how to manage on very little money. That's how 'Family Groups' were initiated. The idea was to invite them into the Community House at a regular time where there'd be a simple activity, like making a cake, or other household skill. In the process, people would talk. A crèche was provided so children could be there too. They were set up on Greenleys and Fullers Slade. There were probably less people leaving Milton Keynes than other new cities because of the Corporation's social development policy.

Norma Jamieson and Carole Loxton

Wedding in Cyprus

I'm still friends with a lot of people from the Community House. We were of a similar age, had similar-aged children, not an awful lot of money, all in the same position. My daughter married a Cypriot, had her wedding in Cyprus,

and about twenty-six people, a lot from Galley Hill, came out for the wedding.

Norah Loh

My parents are a rock

Some of my friends thought it was the back of beyond when I came up to Milton Keynes but my parents – who are a rock and a support – they didn't see it as a problem. It was just up the M1 and they liked the area for us and for the children. They could easily get to us and we to them. We were back to London every week because I depended on my parents for help with the children, but now I see Milton Keynes as home.

Eileen Bowen

Beyond were the brickfields

I was born in Plymouth and my family came to Bletchley in 1965, when I was nine. My first memory of the house was that it was adjacent to the Oxford/Bletchley railway line; beyond that were the brickfields from the London Brick Company. There was an expanse of area to play in, and I remember the flatness of the countryside compared to Plymouth.

Peter Truscott

Now it's a vineyard

I was born in 1931 in Cottage Farm, Woughton, the third generation of Kings to farm here. I took over in 1954 when my father died. Prior to the new city, the farm covered an area we called 'The Patch', which is now a vineyard; also the other side of the canal bridge where Tinker's Bridge estate has been built; Netherfield was five or six fields, and this side of the canal – Woughton Park Estate – was ours as well.

Tony King

Victorian houses in Wolverton, looking north to the railway viaduct and the Works, 1950s.

New homes at Fullers Slade under construction, 1972.

Albert Rose and son in the garden of Railway Terrace, Bletchley, with the embankment and locomotive shed in the background, 1930s.

My brothers would chase hippos

I was born in Tanzania but lived all my life in Uganda. I came to Wolverton in 1972, when we were kicked out by Idi Amin. It was an extended family. My parents used to live with me, my two children and my two brothers and their families. We all lived in a big house – a lovely house on the bank of Lake Victoria. Sometimes my brothers would chase the hippos out of our garden at four in the morning. I used to play hockey and cricket at a very high standard – life was good. When I came to Britain, I came with an open mind because we had no choice. The saddest thing was my parents could not come here; they had to go to India. My two brothers could not

come here because they were stateless – one had to go to America and the other to Canada. My parents had relied a lot on us so the sons used to send them money to keep them going. One of my sisters had to go to Kenya and she is still there. She got married and settled down there. So that is our life.

Ranjeet Toprani

The first tenants in a brand new house

We moved to the city centre in early 1980. We were the first tenants in a brand new house. We only had to get carpets and furniture. We chose the house because we didn't have our own transport. It was better than London. I never felt like going back to London.

Mustafa A. Alami

The rains on Netherfield

The rains on Netherfield were more than a legend – they were a nightmare for people. They were flat roofs and in house after house they leaked. I couldn't believe how badly until I went in on rainy days [as MKDC Community Worker] just to see the water running through the roof. This was clearly an enormous problem because it wasn't just two or three isolated houses. It could be everyone in a long block. The Corporation were concerned and got the builders back to look at this. To be honest, I don't think they had a clue what was happening. They came armed over and over again with great tubes of mastic – I think they masticked the whole building, but it didn't keep the water out. Once the rain started, the mud was everywhere – on people's brand new carpets. Everybody got down great pieces of polythene, or newspapers. Eventually they re-roofed the houses, but it was a terrible experience.

Jeff Fawcett

Building horizontally

I thought Netherfield was quite good for mass housing – it was a reaction to tower blocks because Milton Keynes was a low-density city. Netherfield used exactly the same technique, a way of building quickly, but horizontally rather than building it vertically.

David Stabler

Condensation problems

If you went to the Housing Department because there were terrible condensation problems, they told you to open the windows and turn on the central heating. This seemed a bit daft because heating was expensive and people found it very difficult to cope with.

Lesley Moore

Plenty of space

The houses were an unorthodox design but very well built and had plenty of space. When we built them, they were Parker Morris, a very good standard of housing. You had to provide so many socket outlets and cupboards – things we take for granted, but you don't get them in the private-sector housing, which is a miserable size: families squeezed into little boxes and there's hardly any garden.

Philip Ashbourn

So many things were going wrong

There was more anxiety than excitement when we moved into our new house because so many things were going wrong: the floors weren't satisfactory and the builders had to dig

Coffee Hall houses and Woughton Leisure Centre being constructed, 1979.

New arrivals in Galley Hill, 1979.

those up. The canal had burst its bottom and six miles of it had come over the land so, although it didn't harm the house, the ground was a quagmire. We were picking up freshwater mussels for years afterwards.

Carole Loxton

Keeping families together

People absolutely loved the houses – to the extent that, very often, up came their aunties and the cousins and the grannies. On Oldbrook in particular, a lot of the grandparents were brought up and took houses in sheltered housing. They tried to keep families together in those days.

Norma Jamieson

Very nicely located for family and friends

I can't see us moving from the city. There's plenty to keep us occupied. We're both heading towards retirement so, with that in mind, we're not going to be leaving like some people do – off to the seaside or finding a retirement home. Milton Keynes is very nicely located for family and friends around the country, so we are here to stay.

Ruth Salter

All our lives

I was born in Oxford Street, Wolverton, in 1926. We lived with my grandparents. When my wife and I married, we moved into Western Road and we've lived here ever since. And it's our Golden Wedding next year. One of my sons lives in New Bradwell and one lives in Newport. So four generations of our family have lived in this area all our lives.

Henry Dewick

two

Schooldays
and Training

Bletchley Boys Brigade on parade outside the Lantern Café, 1942.

Wolverton Boys School, late nineteenth century.

Dunce's cap, 1863

I made a dunce's cap for tiresome boys. I am at a loss to find some means to stop them talking.

May Dunmille, Headmistress of Wolverton Infants' School (now Wyvern Infants' School)

Cold, 1870

1 February: It takes us all our time to keep anything like warmth either in ourselves or in the poor children who do nothing but cry and complain of the cold. Their room is more like a barn than anything else. Be the fire ever so large, it never seems to warm the room. We might as well be without one for what good it does.

Adelaide Fielding, Stantonbury Infants' School Logbook

Scolded and refused, 1877

18 July: On coming to school at two o'clock, I was detained some minutes by Mrs Hunt, who wished to speak to me about a book her little boy had taken home from school and which she returned to me. On arriving at the school, I found the manager, the Reverend Mr Harnett, present, who was too angry to listen to hear the reason for my absence and scolded me very much about it. For the future I am to appraise the parents that I am bound to be at school on the stroke of two o'clock.

4 December: Fanny Cummings, now assistant mistress at Calverton, obtained First Class scholarship but is refused an entrance into college owing to her sister having just died of consumption.

Headmistress, Wolverton Infants' School Logbook

The cane, 1884

When I started school at the Church of England School, Church Green Road, Bletchley, I had to cross two fields to get there. Cows grazed in these fields and were a hazard on dark winter afternoons. They seemed so large to a four-year-old. We all had to be in school before the bell in the tower stopped ringing. If we were not, we had a black mark. Persistent latecomers were caned, something which was never spared in my day.

Amy Knill

High school problems, 1890s

23 February 1893: I am sorry to state that some indecent writing was found in the offices one day this week. The writing was removed immediately, I hope before it was seen by any of the girls. I spoke to the elder girls about the matter, but cannot think that any of them would be guilty of such a thing. I believe they are doing their best to find out the culprits – but from the nature of the offence this is of course very difficult.

27 October 1899: Standard V is the worst for attendance. One girl was summoned and fined a fortnight ago and has not been to school since.

May 1901: Miss Belfitt does not get on very well with her class, I am sorry to say. I think the class has great difficulty in understanding what she says, as she speaks in – I presume – the Staffordshire dialect. Her discipline is poor and the class is very noisy and lazy.

Amy Williams,
Headmistress of Stantonbury Girls School

No reflections or opinions, 1904

The logbook should be stoutly bound and contain not less than 300 ruled pages. It must be kept by the Principal Teacher who is required to enter in it such events as the introduction of new books, apparatus or courses of instruction; any plan of lessons approved by the Board; the visits of managers; absence, illness, or failure of duty on the part of any of the school staff; or any special circumstance affecting the school that may, for the sake of future reference or any other reason, deserve to be recorded. No reflections or opinions of a general character are to be entered in the book.

Instructions by the Board of Education
on the keeping of the School Logbook of the
New Wolverton British School, Infants' Department.

Too mechanical, 1909

The full value of the teaching of the infants is prejudiced by its being too mechanical. Too much is done for the children, whose curiosity and intelligence are not being formed. Reading is purely imitative and the same book is read until it is known by heart. Number too is taught from weary rows of figures. I very much wish that the teaching were less noisy. I must add, on the other hand, that there is no lack of zeal or earnestness in the instruction. It only wants redirection and pruning.

F.G. Wood,
Correspondent for the Governors' Report

Excellently taught, 1911

The hymns were sung very sweetly and prayers said reverently. The little ones repeated the Parable of the Sower very nicely. Several texts were repeated without mistake. There is abundant evidence that Scripture has been excellently taught. The children are bright and happy; they have plenty of games and movement and thoroughly enjoy their school life.

Henry Welch and HMI Mr E.C. Streaffield, Board
of Education Report on Wolverton Council School

Infectious disease, 1911-12

12 April 1911: 145 absent.
24 April: 27 new admissions. There are now 270 on registers.
28 April: 129 present. Closed at 12 p.m. by instructions received from Aylesbury. This is owing to the epidemic of measles.

Pupils and teachers in front of the Simpson School, *c*. 1900.

17 July: Two cases of scarlet fever notified – William Young and Bessie Campion.

21 July: Fresh case of scarlet fever – ★William Mackerness, who is subject to fits and has deficient intellect.

24 July: Four fresh cases of scarlet fever – Ethel Funge, ★Duncan Wills, who is delicate and absent months at a time on doctor's orders, William Pratt, Horace Parrott.

(★William Mackerness and Duncan Wills are to be retained in the Infants' Department when they are seven years old in Spring 1912.)

18 March 1912: Two fresh cases of diphtheria – Una Tilley and Harold Foxley.

19 March: Was sorry to hear Harold Foxley died this morning. This is the fifth death from diphtheria in this department since the summer holidays, three of the children having been in Class 2.

25 March: Several fresh cases of whooping cough and chickenpox reported. In this department, 231 children have been affected with infectious disease, with a loss of 7,762 attendances.

Elizabeth Ainge, Headmistress, Infants' Department, Wolverton British School

'Wolverton's Quota to the World's Genius, 1914'

This week is the jubilee of the Science and Arts Institute and its record fifty years of work, with the results of which Wolverton may well be proud. Wolverton has been the centre of engineering interest since the days of the last century when she first became a centre of railway activity. The Institute has trained the minds of four or five generations of Wolverton's sons. All over the world, wherever great engineering and railway industries are linking up the forces of Nature, you will find Wolverton engineers, men who served their apprenticeship in the Works, and who spent their evening hours at the Science and Arts Institute.

Wolverton Express, 29 May 1914

Distractions during the First World War

3 September 1913: The school is a little unsettled in consequence of the large camps situated on the west and east sides of town: the 10th, 11th and 12th Brigades of infantry and a large body of field artillery are encamped for the annual army manoeuvres.

5 March 1915: A Railway Detective called, respecting some boys who had stolen some sweets from the Goods Shed. A boy named George Hickford was the ringleader. He has been troublesome in school this week and ran home this morning at playtime. He presented himself again this afternoon and received special attention. I do not think he will be troublesome again next week.

5 November 1915: Mr Hickson, Mr Watson and Mr Nicholson have now all left to join HM Forces.

31 March 1916: Worst storm I remember on Monday night and continued throughout Tuesday. With the aid of six zinc baths and eight buckets, able to keep back flood water.

H.J. Hippsley, Headmaster, Wolverton Boys' School

Jam and urinals, 1917-22

24 September 1917: Half-day holiday given to enable the children to pick blackberries to be made into jam for the Army and Navy. I have impressed upon the children that they are to go with their mothers or older sisters, as they are too young to go alone.

25 September: The children in this department gathered 32½ lbs of blackberries yesterday afternoon.

15 October: I do not think it advisable for the Infants to have any more blackberrying holidays as so much rain has fallen lately. The grass is very wet. They have been on three half-days and have brought in over 170lbs.

Army manoeuvres in Wolverton, 1913.

11 November 1918: Just before closing time in the afternoon, a crowd of youths forced their way into the school and asked for the children to be released. Several flowerpots were smashed.

28 April 1922: A letter has been sent from Aylesbury, stating that the defect in the floor of the urinals is owing to misuse by the boys. This morning, I have taken each class of boys down to explain how it should be used, although I fail to agree with the statement. I have visited the lavatories frequently to see that they are perfectly used and have often talked to the children on the matter for the last fifteen years.

Elizabeth Ainge, Headmistress,
Infants' Department, Wolverton British School

A typical arithmetic lesson on a cold winter day, 1920s

The schoolmaster at the Bletchley Church of England School, 'Sammy' to us, sat on the top iron guard round the stove, cane nearby, watching his scholars like a hawk. We had been given a sheet of paper and a pencil each, the sums were on the blackboard, a whole boardful, and woe betide anyone who looked elsewhere besides the blackboard and the paper in front of him. After a certain time, we were told to stop. Then we were called out to stand round the master, papers and pencils at the ready. He called out the answers, we ticked those we had correct and put a cross beside those which were wrong. He then collected the papers, tore them across and put them in the stove. End of arithmetic lesson!

George Chandler

Wolverton Works apprenticeship, 1920s

I went on the coach gang to start with. They moved you around, so you don't just get one

man's point of view. As apprentice, I put in fifty-four hours for the first full week. I got five shillings less threepence stoppages. I gave my parents all of it and they gave me back three-pence for pocket money to go to the pictures or a dance. Mr Russell expected me to do a man's work. He'd stop with you for the first week or two and show you how to bend high-pressure pipes and then he'd give you a set of pipes to fit to the cylinders and the filling valve and say, 'Now you do it'. He'd go off doing something else. He'd come back and try them all and if they weren't right, he'd put a saw through them and throw them as scrap and make you do it again. He'd say, 'If a job's worth doing, it's worth doing right!' He was a bit short-tongued and everything had to be right.

Cecil Palmer

Fegan's orphanage, 1920-30s

Fegan's orphanage [in the High Street, Stony Stratford] was started up by Mr J.W.C. Fegan, a businessman who was perturbed by the number of homeless on the streets of London. He sought a country home for them where they could be brought up in the fresh air and instructed in the Christian faith. Mr and Mrs Bennett were superintendents who arrived in 1926 on the tram and were met by an orphanage boy with a wheelbarrow for their luggage. In March 1937, something went wrong with the boilers and the orphanage caught fire.

'NS'

Early howlers

The governor of Fegan's ran a little quiz for the small Stony Stratford boys. Perhaps the questions were a little outside the normal curriculum, but he smiled at some of the answers. For example:

Fegan's boys on a trip from the Stony Stratford orphanage, 1920s.

Drake is the father of ducks.

Rice is a pudding made in China.

N.B. stands for Naughty Boy. It also stands for Northampton Brewery.

The Battle of Waterloo was fought in Trafalgar Square. Nelson led the defeated side.

From *Loving and Serving* by A. Tiffin

Uniform, materials and equipment, 1930s

Greek dancing at York House School [Stony Stratford] was an extra. We took part in leotards around the fishpond which had a lawn area with trees in the centre of a circular driveway. In winter, we had long navy knickers with a pocket for a hankie on the front of one leg. The Head kept hers inside her knicker leg and was always pulling up her skirts searching for it! Winters were very cold – snow would stand three feet high at the side of our road. The school had only one house-fire in the corner of each room and teacher usually stood with her back to it! I had such bad chilblains, all my fingers were covered in bandages. Stationery, textbooks and so on were all extras. From the age of twelve, I was in charge of issuing these out to be put on the bills to parents each term. It cost my father £9 a term for me in fees. Our desks were the 1920s brand – ironwork base, wooden desk, top which lifted, in which to keep books, inkwell at right corner and a wooden seat which lifted up when one had to stand at one's desk. They were designed for two girls to sit together. The school had a large barn for breaktime if wet. We played wooden hoops, skipping and hopscotch.

Audrey Lambert

Class IV of Wolverton School, *c.* 1929. The teacher is Lawrence Oliver Bull, known as LOB. (courtesy of Sidney Horne, front row, second from right)

Evacuees and air raids, 1940s

September 1939: The school opened today to accommodate children evacuated from London on account of war being imminent. Notification has been received from Aylesbury that the school is closed until further notice, except for the use of evacuated children.

April 1940: Fourteen children were admitted this morning, making the number on roll 188. Miss Peacock (London County Council) now has forty-eight evacuees, assisted by Miss Humphries.

June 1940: The roll includes ninety-five children from Chingford.

October 1940: Air-raid warnings today gave rise to considerable congestion in the Infants' School. All the girls from the Girls' School had to be accommodated on the ground floor. Consequently, about 700 children are massed together at a time when dispersal is the one great necessity. The atmosphere was fearful, the strain on the staff enormous.

December 1940: Walls and surface shelters are being built in the playground for protection from air raids. Incidentally, the walls make the school much less draughty and warmer.

7 June 1946: Victory Day was celebrated today. The hall was very gay with flags and bunting and the children enjoyed singing the special songs, saluting the Union Jack and listening to the military and naval marches on the gramophone. The singing of the National Anthem and cheering the King, soldiers, sailors and airmen was done with characteristic enthusiasm and energy.

From the 1939-46 school logs of Miss K. Skinner, Headteacher of Wolverton Infants' School

Staff exams, 1940s

To pass the entrance exam for the staff at the Railway Works, I went to the Science and Arts

Institute evening classes. Later, I went for several years to Mrs Holland in Wolverton Road, who was noted as a teacher of shorthand; typing; economics and railway geography – we had to know every station on the LMS line; principal county towns and the products they were noted for and on which rivers they stood and so on. This was all for the Efficiency Exam to stay on the staff, usually by eighteen years of age.

Audrey Lambert

New tables, tubs and mugs for Infants, 1950s…

Autumn term, 1949: Nursery and equipment fumigated, owing to case of scarlet fever. Cracked and buckling asbestos sheets on walls behind the stores replaced by new sheets.

Autumn term, 1950: New tables and chairs to replace desks. Library books arrived from Aylesbury.

Autumn term, 1951: Diphtheria immunisations. Electric sockets installed in classrooms for use with electric radio set. The set is controlled from a cupboard in the stockroom and the amplifier plugged into the classroom.

June 1953: Tubs outside school planted with Coronation colours: marguerites, geraniums and lobelia. 351 Coronation mugs received. Coronation Bible for the school received. 286 children visited the Palace Cinema to see the Coronation film of Queen Elizabeth II.

From the 1949-53 school logs of Margaret Hiscock, Headteacher of Wolverton Infants' School.

…but still outside toilets

I started school [at the Church of England School, Bletchley] at five, in 1956. The school was very old with outside toilets and just three women teachers.

Rosemary Evans

Discipline, 1960s

I never had any interest in French. One day I was out in the corridor – you know, 'Get out!' – and you used to have stand in the corridor. There were a couple of us out there, giggling and laughing, and the teacher came out and actually slapped my face. In those days, you never dared say anything because you'd go home to Mum and Dad and they'd say, 'You obviously deserved it'. But looking back on it now, he was a strong old boy, he sort of rocked my head back, you know, an open-handed slap.

Stephen Flinn

Everything available to everybody, 1970s

The comprehensive spirit was about and I thought I'd have a go. Got a deputy headship in Huddersfield then became head of Shirebrook Grammar in Derbyshire for a year, to convert it to a comprehensive. Because I was, by then, imbued with a strong feeling that everything should be available to everybody, not chopped up and cut off. I got seconded to the Schools' Curriculum Council for England and Wales which took me all over the world to learn about how things should be done in education. And I was going back to Shirebrook to plough all this deep, profound new knowledge when somebody in a pub said, 'Why don't you apply for that job?' And that was Stantonbury.

Geoff Cooksey

Modern ideas

My oldest daughter was fourteen when we came to Milton Keynes in 1974. She was the first intake at Stantonbury Campus. I knew the teachers through the Drama Group and they had brilliant ideas. I didn't like them being called by their first names though – I thought it made the children have no respect. A lot of children liked it. They had a smoking room – Geoff Cooksey

Wolverton Girls' School, *c*. 1931.

with his modern ideas! They weren't run-of-the-mill teachers. They were very young. The first day, there was no uniform, but Melanie had a uniform so I said she may as well wear it. She had three-quarter socks, grey skirt and maroon blazer. She said, 'Don't ever send me in that thing again'. Some of them went to school as if they were going to a night club. I wasn't happy about Melanie going there. She was more advanced than most of the children. She liked it.

Joan Thompson

Immensely normal

It's always struck me as rather strange that people called Stantonbury Campus radical. It always seemed to us immensely normal. You actually treated children in the same way that you treat your own kids. And you treated parents in the same way that you treat your neighbours. And the school didn't belong to you, it belonged to everybody. And if you're out to get the best out

of life, you could do it by co-operation. And if you wanted people to co-operate then you would use every skill, every trick, every guile to ensure people did co-operate.

Geoff Cooksey

Rewarding and difficult

The kids interviewed me. You had a staff interview and then an interview with the children. They asked me what was my favourite lesson and what I would do to a naughty child. The kids showed me round the school. You sensed it was breaking new ground and that could be either very rewarding or very difficult and the reality was both!

Debbie Greaves

Astounding ignorance

I had awful problems settling into school, being teased rotten, being asked questions like, 'What

The gym at the secondary school, Wolverton, *c.* 1930.

is it like to live in a tree?', 'What is it like to live in the jungle?'. Prior to coming to this country, I don't think I had met any racism. The ignorance was astounding. I remember coming home in tears one day. 'What is the matter?' my mother asked, trying to calm me down. I said, 'He called me a Paki, he said "Paki go home".' 'Who did?', she asked. I said, 'A West Indian boy'. I totally missed the irony as a child, but my mum laughed.

Soraya Billimoria

Liking learning

My family moved to Milton Keynes when I was eight. I was the only Chinese person in my whole school at first, which was quite challenging – there was racism sometimes. At fourteen, I had problems with English because it wasn't my first language. I speak fluent Cantonese and understand a little Mandarin, but I speak to my parents in Chinese as a sign of respect. I've liked everything about learning. I went to college for two years and university for three years, studying sociology. Now I work for the Racial Equality Council, providing a necessary service in Milton Keynes.

Mabel Kong

Learning to stand back

You became an arrivals worker [for MKDC in the 1970s] by answering an ad, passing the interview and going on a training course. You needed people skills. 'Enabling' was a word used a lot. You had six weeks on-the-job training with other community workers. You needed a good listening ear, and to be able to communicate well. You had to be discreet and have integrity. There was some formal training, like report writing. Learning to stand back and let others take over was really important.

Norma Jamieson and Carole Loxton

Children learning about building for the future at the Milton Keynes Urban Studies Centre, 1980s.

Winners of the flower show at Bushfield School, 1982.

three
Working Life

Wolverton Works employees, 1913: flat hats were worn by the workers, bowler hats by the Foremen, and the 'trilby' hat by the Manager.

The foreman in his bowler hat

My father was a chargehand with apprentices working under him. His money was very good, over £2 a week. It's all different to what it is today. There was no standard wage. The foreman used to go to work in a bowler hat. His wages were vastly different to the journeyman/mechanic. They never did any actual work. They'd stand around and see that everyone was doing their job right. But he was a skilled man himself, he could do the work too. There were 5,000 employees when I was there. We didn't see the managers very often. They'd just walk round and then they'd go up to the top offices.

Cecil Palmer

The smith's shop

The smithy at the Wolverton Works is a very fine building, 350 feet long and 90 feet wide. There are seventy fires, including three crane fires for heavy work and fifteen oil furnaces for the drop hammers, forging presses and so on. Fourteen steam hammers are laid down, five of 15cwt each. Work is found here for 288 men and lads.

From *A Guide to Wolverton Works*, 1906

No bank accounts

People in the early days didn't have bank accounts, as their pay packets were spent when they got them – on rent, coal and electric and so on.

Ron Perry

Basic slag

We used basic slag as a manure for the land – it releases its nutrients very slowly over a period of years. It's not a manure that can bleach from the ground like phosphates, nitrogen and potash. If you use too much of that, you may as well throw your pennies down the drain.

Bernard Groom

Horses for harrowing

We done mixed farming – sheep, cows, pigs, poultry, corn – on 265 acres. We had a horseman, cowman, cowman's assistant, chaps that looked after the sheep. One field was called Bloody Bork: years ago, two fellers had a fight with poles in that field and one was killed. Then there was Sheltermore, Common Field, Ten Acres, Top Hills, Furzton Field, Hovel Field and Rushy Slad and Little Slad – very boggy. Texas Homecare was built right in the middle of a field we called Rooksley. We'd find big flints but, in those days, they weren't so collectable as they are now. The man that looked after the horses would cart mangolds and swedes in the winter, from Bradwell – food for the dairy cows. We'd use the horses for harrowing the corn in, after we'd drilled it with a tractor.

David Bodley

An acre in a day

In January, we kept off the land when it was wet – this clay land set hard. January was mostly a muck-carting job month. February was hedge-laying. Then come March we could get on the land a bit. If you had a pair of horses, you'd do ever so well to do an acre in a day.

Lol King

Returned to service

At the beginning of November, we usually run one ram to about sixty ewes, but sometimes you get an infertile ram, and you can't risk losing your lamb crop through a chap who

Wolverton Works, *c*. 1900.

can't do his job, so you put two in. We put on ravels – a leather harness to go on the rams, fits on the chest. We put a red marker on these at Simpson – they should lamb within the first three weeks of March. Then when we take those rams out, we'll put different rams in with a different colour, so that we can tell if any of those particular females have what we call 'returned to service'.

Sam and Pam Sinfield

Job for a wet day

My father did all the work with horses and bred his own. He always had a couple of mares and foals around. We had shire horses. We'd take them into Fenny Stratford to a blacksmith's shop. That was always a job for a wet day. If you couldn't do anything else, you'd set off to Bletchley with a horse to get some shoes for it.

Tony King

Boat-building at Stony

Hayes Wharf was where they built boats in Stony Stratford. I saw the boats launched side-ways into the canal in Wharf Lane at Old Stratford. They built the boats and took them on a trailer to Old Stratford, drawn by a steam engine, on a cradle. As the boat was launched, all the water shot out of the canal. They took them boats right through to Cosgrove until they got them onto the Grand Union Canal and away through to London. They had all been fitted up at the works, and then dismantled so they could get through the locks. The men used to go up to London to fix it up – putting the funnels on and so on – ready for going abroad. There was about 50 to 100 people employed there.

Cecil Palmer

Horseradish and milk

Mrs Hack lived in an old house in Stony Stratford High Street. She earned pin money by scraping horseradish. Anyone who lives at the bottom end of town will know it grows like a weed. A little factory up Wolverton Road, next door to the Duke of Edinburgh, used to mince it up to make the horseradish

cream. Mr Eales was the first milkman in town to deliver his milk in bottles. He had twelve bottles in all. He'd fill six of them from the churn, put them in the wire rack of his bicycle, cycle round the town and deliver them, collect the empties, bring them back home, wash them, fill them up. It was a lengthy process – he was often seen still delivering at eleven o'clock at night!

'NS'

Travelling traders

Mr Lines and Mr Dolling both came with their milk floats from Shenley each day. They had churns in the back with measures hanging in them. People went out with jugs to get them filled. There was often a nice pile of horse manure in the street and I was dispatched by

Ivor Brown, of Anson Road, Wolverton, helping with the Co-op milk round, c. 1929.

mother, complete with bucket and small shovel, to collect this, which she put round her rose trees. A man would come up the backways calling 'Line props!', and the knife-grinder called to sharpen scissors, knives, garden shears.

Audrey Lambert

Cowley's bakers

My parents never had a holiday, always hard-working – early in the morning to produce the bread, then the afternoons to deliver it round the district. I've been out till midnight delivering it. In Grandfather's time, we got the flour from Roger's Mill at Stratford. If you were a tradesman and went to pay your bill at the grocer's, they always gave you a glass of wine. They'd run your bill on for weeks and weeks. We had no end of customers who only paid once a year. One of the blacksmiths used to have his bread and we'd get the horse shod, and about once a year we settled up.

Arthur Cowley

Gramp's greengrocery

When I was about nine, we'd grow potatoes and peas, put them in little sacks and send them up to Covent Garden. Peas, brussels, cauliflower – then me Grandad started off on a greengrocery round. Me old Gramp had the old pony and milk float and he'd go round the street selling cabbages at sixpence a piece. He put 'William Willis' on the trolley so everyone thought it was Gramp's business, but it wasn't, it was Teddy Norman's. They thought, 'Oh, he's a poor old pensioner, we'll buy off him'. I used help Gramp with the greengrocery round. At Christmas he'd have variegated holly and cut bits off a fir tree and sell them as Christmas trees.

Joseph Willis

Horrendous dust

I worked at Metallin's in Fenny Stratford in the 1960s, a division of Reckitt's Colours. It's been razed to the ground now, but there was something in the local paper about the extremely high levels of cadmium in the soil making it really dangerous, and we worked there! It was appalling. You had to sieve the colour – cadmium was used in the process. It came in lumps and had to be sieved to make it into a fine powder – the dust was horrendous.

Wendy Marshall

Taste the sulphur

The brickyards were a big employer at Newton Longville and down at Stewartby. They were the last thing anyone wanted to do. I was never going to work in the brickyard. I'd see my father come home coughing and spluttering covered in brick dust, day in day out. He was never a fit man when he worked there. This time of year, it was terrible. On a summer's day, you could taste the stuff in the air, the sulphur.

Alan Marshall

Lumps of meat

I worked at Scot Meats. We were sticking lumps of meat into a pot, shoving it into an oven, pulling it out, wrapping it up and sending it onto a wagon. You didn't have to have a brain to do the job, as long as you could read a dial to make sure that the oven got to the right temperature and you could read the clock for the length of time it had to be in.

Ken Beeley

Liable to be dismissed

My attention has been called to the growing practice of the men leaving their work at

The Scot meat factory in the 1970s when it was one of Bletchley's largest employers, with over 1,000 staff. The factory has now closed.

mealtimes before the whistle blows. This is against the rules and must be stopped. If my attention is again called to any man leaving his work before the proper time, he will hold himself liable to be dismissed.

C.A. Park, Superintendent, Wolverton Works,
7 July 1898

Now I'm for it

I'd go and do the grinding at Watling Street nearly every day. So this particular day, I went up the barn – it was all cobbled – took the tractor in, backed it back to the hammer mill, lined it up by the belt. Then you had to go upstairs, walk along the loft across a plank into another barn to get your stuff, carry it across to put into the hopper at the top so it would mill. So I got it set there going beautiful, carrying this stuff across, then I thought there was

a smell of rubber. I went down and I hadn't set the belt right. It had run over the tractor wheel, brand new tyre and it had cut through the tyre. I thought, 'Oooh hell, now I'm for it'. But what I done, I got some dirt and smeared over it and, do you know, they took them wheels off several times while I was there and they never did find it.

Joseph Willis

Not sufficiently careful

I regret to have to report that James Waterworth, a lad employed as a brass cleaner at London Road, was accidentally killed by being knocked down by a light engine on the 16th ult. as he was returning from the yard after cleaning brake-work. There does not appear to be any blame attached to anyone and the boy unfortunately contributed to his death by not being sufficiently careful. An inquest was held on the boy and a verdict of accidental death returned. I have submitted a letter received from his mother, asking for some assistance.

C.A. Park, Superintendent, Wolverton Works,
7 July 1898

Dreamt of leaving

My parents came to Milton Keynes in around the 1960s. They ran a Chinese restaurant in partnership. I came here to study in 1973. At first, I felt strange because my English was not good, so I found it difficult to communicate with local people. When my father started running the Chinese takeaway in 1977, I stopped studying and started work in there. I have been working for twenty-three years. Working in the takeaway is a hard job. Usually, I start working at noon till two o'clock then I will have two hours' short break. Later on, I will start another section from four o'clock until midnight. I work twelve hours a day. Due to the long working hours, I have no social life at all. I dreamt about going out and making a fresh attempt in another field, but this takeaway is our family-owned business. It is not easy to find someone else to replace my work.

Wai Kau Chan

Chewing and chewing

We had a field of flax, linseed – terrible stuff that is. You shut the cattle out the field when you come through, and pick up all the odd bits of flax that fell off the trailer. If the cattle get that, they keep chewing and chewing and chewing and it went like a ball of string and they couldn't swallow it.

Joseph Willis

Canteen at Wolverton Works, 1986. (photograph by David Runnacles)

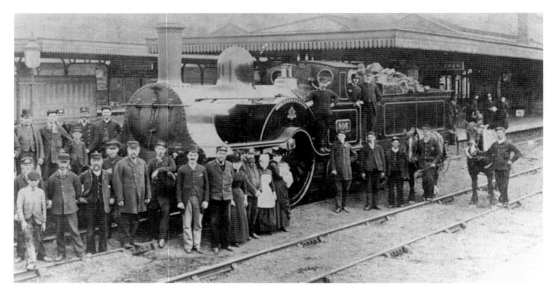

Bletchley station staff with the *Waverley*, no. 806, in 1904. The engine took part in the 1888 Euston to Crewe race, covering 158 miles at an average speed of 53.25 mph.

Market's closed

We normally sell the lambs at market in Northampton or Banbury. Bletchley was a market town – where Sainsbury's is was our market. It transferred to Leighton Buzzard, but it's not worth going to because there's few there. There's a market at Winslow on Tuesdays. That's about it. Olney's closed, Aylesbury market's closed, Northampton is moving out to Blisworth. Market sites are nearly always owned by the borough, and are in the middle of the town – the land is more valuable for building.

Sam and Pam Sinfield

Shops closed

Since the new city came, practically all the shops [in Stony] closed down. The people that were running them were getting old and the younger ones could see no business coming into the town now they've made this Loop road [1978]. You've got to rely on the old townspeople or these few that come down from Galley Hill and

Fullers Slade. When they get their own shops up there, they won't come into town.

Cecil Palmer

Shops opened

When I came here in 1974, I started looking for a shop in Milton Keynes but it had just started and there were only about fifteen or twenty villages round about. To start a shop is not that easy – it was easy in Kenya, because you had a lot of support from relatives. Now our Asian community have made themselves felt as part and parcel of the place. They are very well assimilated and settled in Milton Keynes.

Ratilal Hirji Shah

Pushed about

My shop is in Queensway, Bletchley. When CMK opened, most of the shops shut and we lost business. I do not like it at all. I have been there only about fifteen times. When you walk here, you walk freely. When you go there, you are pushed about.

Francesco Russo

Decadence

After working in Ghana for VSO, the decadence of Milton Keynes is overwhelming. There was a big Budgens in central Milton Keynes. I remember going there not long after I came back and standing in tears in one of the aisles because I couldn't decide. In Ghana you had no choice. You had onions, tomatoes, peppers, maybe some rice from the street markets. In Budgens I wanted washing powder and there were thirty different options!

Debbie Greaves

Proper dinners

I worked for a site agent when the city started. I used to do their dinner, all the agents and the office staff. A chap transported me to Bradwell and Wolverton to get food, then I'd come back and cook it. I'd do proper vegetables and hotpot, proper dinners they got and a sweet. All the huts were constructed on site. I had a little kitchen with a proper wooden floor. It was nice. We'd have site meetings there and I'd get my tray out and they had their tea and biscuits. A lot of them lived on that site and used to go home on weekends. Some had caravans and some had little wooden dormitories. They were very nice people. They came from the Oldham area mainly. Ever such nice men, ever so gentle. I think they appreciated what we did. They'd come back covered in mud because they'd go under these tunnels [for the balancing lake] on skates. Some of these tunnels were twenty-five foot. They had to go flat down them in their skates and they were covered in water. It was amazing.

Sandra Page

Terrified

I was straight out of college. I'd failed my London Chamber of Commerce secretary's certificate because I'd spent the night up partying the night before and actually went to sleep in the middle of the exam. I never took to shorthand. I arrived at the Milton Keynes Development Corporation and within a week I was told that all the secretaries had to take it in turns to minute the Corporation Board Meeting, and of course my shorthand was totally useless. I was absolutely terrified. I arrived at the assigned time. They said, 'We should have a rogues' gallery of all the Board Members so you know who to attribute which remark to'. They'd lost the photographs. Anyway, I went in with my shorthand notepad and everybody was pouring over maps. Great big Board table and they'd all got their bottoms in the air, looking at the maps and mumbling. I hadn't a clue what was going on so I took a few notes and typed them up and sent them in. I never heard any more about it. I didn't get asked to do it again.

Sue Malleson

Very uncomfortable

I worked at Kiln Farm in one of the Advance Factory Units. Very uncomfortable buildings they were – just a metal shell, extremely hot in summer and as the metal expanded in the sun, it cracked and made terrible noises. In winter, they were extremely cold. We often worked wearing gloves and coats indoors, but, as hardy land surveyors, we were expected to put up with this sort of thing. It didn't help that we shared the building with the Soils Laboratory, who constantly had the back doors open with vehicles arriving, bringing samples of soil.

Malcolm Anderson

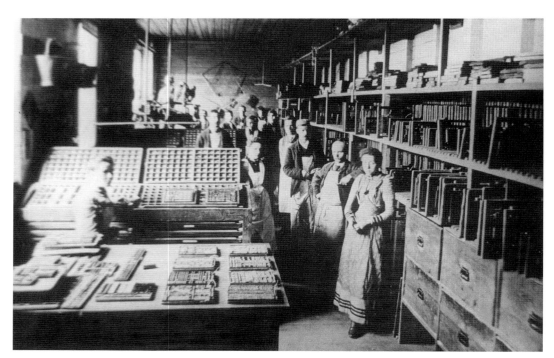

Above: The composing room at McCorquodale's printers, Wolverton, *c.* 1905. *Below:* McCorquodale's in the 1940s.

Managing it for the city

There was a bit in the middle of the Bletchley industrial area that was the biggest mess we took on. We got people to repaint their factories, to plant trees and shrubs, just to brighten it up a bit. A wonderful guy, Richard Pinkham – he's eighty-something now – joined our little group and he was seen by the tenants to be an absolute little Hitler from the Corporation who used to come and nag them furiously to keep their premises looking OK. If you go to Kiln Farm now, all the verges are parked on. It's a complete mess. There was none of that when we were managing the properties. You didn't think, 'This is just a property investment, I must only maximise the value of my investment'. You were managing it for the city. That's a fundamental difference, but with probably a better outcome for the investment!

Bob Hill

A state of decline

The landscape and the ecology were pretty ropy. The farming at the time had changed to arable. Hedgerows had been planted for the maintenance of stock but the heavy ground was increasingly used for cereal growing. So the fields were pretty devoid of anything approaching interest in wildlife terms. The odd partridge and pheasant, that was about it. Wildlife was confined to the hedgerows and ponds. And the hedgerows were predominantly elm – something like 350 miles of hedgerow in Milton Keynes, and with the prospect of Dutch elm disease, we were going to lose most of it. The ash trees too were in a state of decline, the subject of a national study at the time. One of my first jobs as Forestry and Conservation Officer was the felling and disposal of 50,000 mature elms.

Brian Salter

Do your best

I worked as a dinner lady in Emerson Valley. Then I was singled out by the headteacher to work as a clerical assistant. I was very happy to be given the chance. The vernacular of English and the accent is very difficult compared to the formal English I learned in Hong Kong. The headteacher really helped. After that, I worked for Milton Keynes Council and undertook some translation work for the Mayor. I can speak several province languages. I received personal thanks from the Mayor, but my colleagues were not happy – they thought I was showing off. There is a difference in our cultures and our personal ethos. I think that if you are earning money from somewhere then you should do your best for them.

Helen Cheuk

It wasn't an ordinary job

I'd cycle up to the city on the Redway with the children. I worked for the Milton Keynes Development Corporation, in the Library – I could take the children in with me. MKDC was one of the few organizations that allowed that. They had their own temp register. You'd go in and tell them what you could do, and they'd try and place you by the end of the week. I worked on the opening of the Peace Pagoda. MKDC had a caravan at the site. It was very muddy, but like a hospitality suite. I had to make tea for everyone – Frank Henshaw [MKDC General Manager] and the Mayor. There was also an elephant. I don't know where that came from, but it loved tea. Every now and then its trunk would appear round the door of the caravan and I'd give it a cup of tea. It wasn't an ordinary job!

Maralyn Tamblin

Bletchley's Watling Street Industrial Estate, 1974, before refurbishment by MKDC and tenants.

Wolverton's Royal Train crews. From left to right: Buddy Abbott (fireman), Harry Bolton (driver), Bert Goodman (driver), Alf Johnson (fireman).

The best job

I came to Milton Keynes purely by chance. I opened the Architects' Journal and it said, 'Would you like to be part of a team building a new city?'. It changed my life. I was in MKDC for twenty-two years. I wasn't bored once. I was excited most of the time. I got into marketing and that was wonderful. It's the best job I've ever had in my life.

David Stabler

four

Entertainment and Leisure

The original Red Balloon Day, 1982, used for an MKDC television advertisement for Milton Keynes which said, 'Wouldn't it be nice if all cities were like Milton Keynes?'

Late starter

At the age of thirty-six, I started playing in a rhythm and blues band. Fantastic. I was always a late starter.

Tracy Walters

The Beatles – live

As a teenager, I'd go to the Palace Ballroom. Billy Fury, Brenda Lee, The Animals, The Searchers, The Hollies – they all came to Wolverton. I also saw The Beatles – live – at the ABC cinema in Northampton.

Pat Old

Diana Ross and The Supremes

I joined the Tamla Motown Appreciation Society when I was fifteen and remember meeting Diana Ross and The Supremes, The Marvelettes, The Temptations. They'd send out invites to members of the fan club and you'd go and meet them, get their autographs and chat with them. I went up to the recording of a television programme, *The Sound of Motown*. Dusty Springfield hosted it. There was Dunstable, The California – always really big, Stevie Wonder, Marvin Gaye, The Four Tops and Ike and Tina Turner.

Stephen Flinn

Mudslides and swarms

The Milton Keynes Bowl used to be a Fletton's Brick Pit, 120 feet deep – a bloody great hole in the ground, ideally suited for utilising spoil from the big housing areas being developed – Netherfield, Coffee Hall, Bean

Woughton Choir at a choral festival in Great Brickhill, 1888.

A packed crowd at the Milton Keynes Bowl, 1983.

Hill. We kept going, to build the amphitheatre shape. The first event was Soul in the Bowl in 1979 then, in 1981, Police – notorious because of the mudslides – then Thin Lizzy. 1983 was the big one: David Bowie for three days on the trot. The sun blazed down and every rule in the book was broken about capacities, with the Bowl just looking like a swarm of bees – people everywhere.

Brian Salter

Dancing at Bletchley Park

Friday 24 December 1944: Up early! Didn't do very much work. Played postman. Did some more cards. Everyone very gay. Excitement running high! To dance by 8.15 p.m. No band until 9 p.m! Then some dance. American band and Michael! Great fun. All enjoyed ourselves. Staggered back about 12.30 a.m. Partook of some cheering 'cheer'.

Mavis Faunch

Bombarded by disco requests

I used to fill in as a peripatetic youth worker, doing discos for youth clubs, Scouts, Guides – and parents, who were picking up children from discos. It went from one extreme to another. For fifteen years, my main discos were for the schools, a good eighty-odd in Milton Keynes. It started off maybe twenty a year, then it went to forty or fifty. By the time I finished, I was bombarded – I had to turn people away. They'd book me from one Christmas to another. At the end of term in July, I was doing two or three in a day. I didn't charge a lot of money. I personally feel I've given a service, and I know that the schools, the clubs, the parents, the kids I've come across over the years – I know they feel the same way.

Leroy Clarke

You dance even

We sort of entertained ourselves at home because, as West Indians, when you meet friends you go to houses, you eat, you drink, you talk, you laugh, you dance even sometimes. So you didn't need other outlets.

Eileen Bowen

Great people for parties

The British have a fantastic sense of humour. To understand it as a foreigner, as I am, you had to become one of them before you understand it. They are great people for parties.

Donato Piselli

Treasured and talked about

The Bletchley Show became nationally famous. Special trains ran from the north and south. People came on foot, bicycle, pony trap and horseback. There were sheepdog trials, horse-jumping, tennis tournaments, flower shows, funfairs, athletics, tugs-of-war, floodlit dancing, a brass band playing throughout, and a gigantic, spectacular fireworks display. To Old Bletchley residents, it was the most excit-

ing day of the year, treasured and talked about for many a day afterwards.

Ivy Fisher

Recognized and valued

We set up a charity, The People's Press of Milton Keynes – local books by local people, using the proceeds of one book to pay for the next. Within six weeks, we sold 1,000 copies of the first book, *Piano and Herrings* by Bill Elliott of Wolverton. It was a way for people to be recognized and valued, and not be forgotten.

Roger Kitchen

Tar balls rolling

On Guy Fawkes Day, the students from Hayes Wharf made tar balls. They'd get layers of sacking soaked in tar, roll it up, put wire netting round it, then they'd take it onto the London Road on top of the hill and light it. It would roll down the hill and down the High Street. The policeman would come round and all the students would dodge round a corner. They'd kick it down to Market Square or the Green, where it would burn itself out.

Cecil Palmer

Floor rushes and the fire-eater

Early on in the new city, we had the Milton Keynes Medieval Society. The men used to make chain mail. They wanted us to do some medieval music. The first medieval feast we had was in Fenny Stratford – an old community hall. They brought rushes to put on the floor. We ate off trestles and big platters of bread. There were candles and a fire-eater as well. When I think of the rushes, the candles and the fire-eater – if the Fire Officer

A bonfire at Wolverton, 1907.

had walked in, that would have been the end of it!

Sue Malleson

Carnival at Bletchley

There used to be a good carnival in Bletchley; all the firms put floats in.

Gordon Ridgeway

The fair at Stony Stratford

At the fair [in August], the steam engines and horses used to line up along Horsefair Green and down Silver Street. They weren't allowed on the Square until six o'clock before Fair Day, then they were allowed two days and had to be gone by half-past ten on Sunday morning.

Arthur Cowley

I thought he was dead

A Christmas Carol was performed one year in the Stony Stratford Public Hall and I remember being quite frightened when Scrooge – Mr Benbow, the baker – fell flat on his face and the scenery showed a tombstone. I really thought he was dead!

Audrey Lambert

Goings-on

The Bletchco Players were originally members of the Co-op. Things went on in that group, sinful goings-on. It was a disgrace, but they did put on some good plays, all amateurs. I can't really tell tales as some are still around. The goings-on were between married people, some now pillars of society! I'd help out backstage. There were goings-on there too.

Meg Bates

Fantastic collaboration

I was not the sort who'd ever had anything to do with the theatre. I went along to see *All Change* at Stantonbury. It was in the round – quite remarkable for me. It had this amazing range of people and there was music, some of it really tuneful – all original. The audience were the people I see around Wolverton, again not normally the theatre-going audience. So it made a big impression on me. We did *Days of Pride*, *The Jovial Priest*, *Sheltered Lives* and each one was getting bigger – *Sheltered Lives* had ninety-eight in the cast and backstage! They were fantastic – two, three generations all working together, collaborating, a kind of joyous celebration of community. OK, we don't live in villages any more, but I think we've got something here other people haven't got. It is special.

Roger Kitchen

Rip-roaring success

I have mixed views about the Milton Keynes Theatre. It's marvellous to be able to go to a sort of West-End-style theatre in the middle of the city and it's been a rip-roaring success and it's done wonders for the reputation of Milton Keynes, but I wonder what the cost of it is to community projects. But it is a lovely building.

Ruth Salter

The County and the Studio

The County cinema in Bletchley closed – I think fleas overtook it. It was derelict almost, but larger than the Studio. If there was a popular film you'd queue all round the building to get in. And if you wanted to see a film more than once, you'd just go in and stay there. You'd open the fire doors at the bottom and let your mates in through the window.

Gordon Ridgeway

The Electra

The Electra in Newport Pagnell – the fleapit – was a beautiful place. I don't know if it used to be a dance hall but there were iron railings around part of the seating. Red velvet seats worn thin and little old ladies that sold you the tickets and your sweets and showed you to your seat with a torch.

Annie Bradstock

No smoking…later

In the early days we'd go to the cinema at Newport Pagnell – the most wonderful place on earth. So bizarre! One night, they'd just introduced no smoking and I hadn't seen these signs – about one inch high in the pitch black. I lit up a cigarette and all of a sudden there was a torch in my face and Miss Salmon was saying, 'You're not allowed to smoke in here any more'. I said, 'Oh no! I'm awfully sorry, I didn't know – I'll put it out.' She said, 'You might as well finish it now you've started.'

Sue Burrows

Chewing tobacco

The old farm workers used to chew the old twist of tobacco, like a stick of liquorice. They'd chew that while they were hoeing the weeds in the mangolds or the swedes and then keep spitting the juice out. Or they'd smoke Woodbines or clay pipes.

David Bodley

Jugs of beer

There were about twenty pubs in Stony. I never had a drink of beer until I was seventeen and that was when I was haymaking. You'd got the jugs of beer – there was no tea and no water. I was that dry. They said, 'We've got

Finale of *The Jovial Priest*, produced by the Living Archive at Stantonbury Theatre in 1986.

Roy Nevitt, producer and director of Community Theatre in Milton Keynes since 1972.

The Toc H Rag Handlebar Moustache competition, which was held when *Three Men in a Boat*, starring Jimmy Edwards, was shown at Wolverton's Empire Cinema in the 1950s.

nothing here. You'll have to go home if you want a drink of water. Have a drop of beer'. So I had a drop of beer and I've had a drop ever since.

Cecil Palmer

Very lonely

When I arrived, I felt very ill at ease in Milton Keynes. I didn't know how to connect with the community. As a single woman, it's difficult just to pop down the pub and make yourself known, so that first week was very lonely and very difficult.

Debbie Greaves

No others

Sometimes I tell my wife I am going down the road for a drink. Then I look in the pub and there is no other black person, so I get back in the car and go straight to Luton, to my friends.

Neville Rose

We made friends

We made friends. One or two were local, but the majority were London people. They mixed all right, no messing about. They had a little clubhouse down the Shoulder of Mutton – Yeomanry Hall. You'd have bingo, a pint of beer – all you wanted. There was only one bus from

Bletchley and it stopped there. It was all walking and biking. Nobody had cars. One in a million had a car. We'd take the bus down to the railway station, get the train to Bedford, go on the boats. Used to take the children nearly every other weekend, on the river. Nice, good day.

Ronald Flinn

The Bletchley Town Band

You could walk from Bletchley Road to Western Road. There were rose gardens, tennis courts, and a putting green. There used to be a bandstand on the Leon Recreation Ground and the Bletchley Town Band played there. My grandfather was in the band.

Monica Austin

Spring at Bletchley Park

Tuesday 4 April 1944: Hectic rumours re. cancel of leave. Went back to work for a while after supper – success on the production line! Glorious evening. Cycled back through Old Bletchley – a very brooding atmosphere over everything – maybe it's me. Wonder whether anything will happen? Couldn't write, so talked!

Wednesday 5 April 1944: Rumours confirmed – all leave cancelled – days off OK but no travel permitted – and I'd put in my leave pass for Thursday week! Everyone amazingly cheerful. Thank goodness for the spring. April showery.

Mavis Faunch

Everything from flamingos

If you create the habitat, then the flora and fauna will take advantage of it. We've had everything, from flamingos escaped from wildlife parks to an albatross. Over 200 species of birds have been sighted at Willen.

Brian Salter

Pigeons and poultry

One of my great-uncles kept racing pigeons. These he let fly each evening and they circled in a flock around the rooftops. When he raced them, they were put in a special basket and dispatched by rail from Wolverton to their starting point. I had two holidays when I worked for the local farmer for a week each year and, in return, he delivered a sack of corn to my mother for the poultry.

Audrey Lambert

Big mugs

We used to go trainspotting at Bletchley. There was a good station buffet – big mugs.

Alan Marshall

A missed opportunity

Bradwell Public Bathing Place will be opened on Saturday and the challenge race between the Reverend Guest and Mr Sid Cook of Newport Pagnell has so boomed the occasion that, given a fine day, a tremendous crowd is expected. What a pity Bradwell and Wolverton did not combine to make a place worthy of the 14,000 people who live in the neighbourhood! Neither bathing place is good enough for the requirements of such a large industrial centre and voluntary effort, however praiseworthy, falls short of the crying need for a safe, clean and cooling dip in the refreshing water. It is not an ideal place and there is too much mud about and the river depth is shockingly uneven but human ingenuity and human efforts may do much. Hope on, hope ever.

The *Bucks Advertiser and Aylesbury News*,
26 August 1916

Queen's Pool, Bletchley

I remember the Queen's Pool next door to the cinema. Everything we went to was raising

Bletchley Leisure Centre being built, 1974.

money for the pool. It was open air to start with and got covered later. It was built in gardens, which was one of the nicest parts of Bletchley. We all thought it was terrible when the Leisure Centre was built over them.

Monica Austin

Mr Pratt's rule

The Stony Stratford Bathing Place was overseen by Mr Pratt, who insisted it was the girls one night, the boys another night. He thought it was beyond the limit of men's endurance to see girls stripped off like that.

'NS'

Scrumping

There used to be a big old country house at Holme Chase with a deserted swimming pool and orchards. We always used to go scrumping there.

Stephen Flinn

Run for the hell of it

We'd play in Linford Wood and Downs Barn in 'haunted houses' – empty farmhouses. We had boundaries. If the locals from New Bradwell crossed our boundary, we'd say, 'What are you doing in our fields?'. The same for Wolverton. Our boundary went from Abbey Farm, where the bottom of the golf course is, right up to the A5 to Loughton,

The 'largest model airport in the world', set up in Middleton Hall, CMK, 1982.

back round Old Bradwell Common, then back towards Old Bradwell. Linford Wood was our territory. It was very dense there. Of course, there were notices up, 'Trespassers will be prosecuted', all round the woods. There was a little woodkeeper's hut right in the middle of it – I think it was a toilet for the gentry, because there was a pipe going from it. We'd look for the keeper, get behind him, make a lot of noise and then just run, for the hell of it. We'd go bird-nesting, climbing up trees – see how far you could go without coming down to the ground again.

Jack Stephenson

Nobody would know a thing

I was rebellious when I was at school, such a naughty little girl. I wanted to hang out with my friends after school. They'd all go out with the boys, to the park. I wanted to be part of the crowd. I didn't want to be left out. I'd lie to my

Stantonbury Sunday School outing on the canal, *c.* 1910.

mum and dad and say I was going to my friend's house to study, but really I would be going to the park and sitting on the swings with the girls and some boys. The girls would sit there and smoke. I tried smoking and I just didn't like it. At the age of fifteen, I'd go clubbing. I'd dress myself up. I'd go out in casual gear and take a rucksack with me then change at my mate's house – nobody would know a thing.

Anon

Sardines and metal animals

The Scout Quarries was popular with the Cubs for a day out – we walked each way taking a picnic tea. It was then very wild with many bushes and popular games were Sardines, Spacemen, Robin Hood or Red Indians – everyone made their own bows and arrows. The Scout hats often had floppy brims but to stiffen

them when at camp, they would be left on the roof of the tent at night – the dew straightened them up – or a milk bottle with hot water would be used on a dampened hat. Hooton's Bazaar used to have the whole of the inside room of Wolverton Market. Mother would give me a penny to choose a metal animal and in this way I built up a farmyard and a zoo.

Audrey Lambert

Pocket money

You'd get about a halfpenny or a penny a week pocket money. You'd get a stick of 'Spanish' (liquorice) for a farthing. If you wanted to go to the pictures, you'd get round your father and ask him for another penny. We had to go to Wolverton for the pictures. There wasn't one in Stony in 1910.

Cecil Palmer

Cross-country races

The National Cross Country [race] came across the farm where I was, and the secondary school used to have their cross-country with the children and finish up at the farm there. They were gone quite a long time. We'd clean our copper out down the scullery and boil the water in it to make the tea for them. We'd do it for the sports too. The church once brought the kiddies up for Sports Day and they put swings on the oak trees for them.

Joseph Willis

Fun Days

We started off [in 1988] with a Teddy Bears' Picnic – that was the mums and tods and the playgroup and a lot of youngsters from the National Children's Homes group. And we had a week of events – a sports day, a Saturday fun day – that was a huge success, really superb, and it still goes on now annually.

Norma Jamieson

A smashing gallery

As a qualified youth worker, I could make outreach contact as well as doing adventure playground work. I built a 'smashing gallery' for any kid who wanted to get anger out of them. There'd be all this crockery in a safe environment and they could smash the hell out of anything they liked. It worked really well. We had a graffiti wall which they were allowed to put graffiti on. It was great because they washed it off themselves. In the end, they hated it – it was 'Put up what you like there, you've got to live with it and you've got to wash it off later!'

Tina Strutton

Instant community

The first thing we got through our door was a card asking us if we wanted to be involved with the community centre at Greenleys – you know, meet the rest of the residents. They'd formed a football team – was I interested in being involved? Well, I just joined the club and you've got an instant community – brilliant. I'm still friends with 90 per cent of those people now. And Greenleys were the best team in Milton Keynes for twenty years.

John Staniland

Controversial contributions

Community newspapers were a big thing: Fishermead and Oldbrook had the *Oggie Post* and the *Cornish Pastie Post*. There were lots of ads and information in these papers, all delivered free by volunteers on the estates. Some people made controversial contributions aided by the Community Workers. It was ironic – MKDC funded the Workers, who in turn encouraged people to publish things against the MKDC. There was a lot of anxiety about [conflicting] roles.

Carole Loxton

Blah, blah, blah

A chairman often overdoes it because they are so big-headed and so used to being in charge. After a while, there is a coup because people gain in confidence as they take over. We had the initial meeting of this Community Association and I took the chair as a kind of interregnum before they took elections. I did it sitting on the edge of the table and inviting people's comments on things – what they were hoping for, what they thought the problems were, what they'd like to see, blah, blah, blah. We came to the elections and this person is elected and we change places. This person moves to the table and – bang, bang, bang, 'Order! ORDER!' – and I think, 'Time to move on.'

Roger Kitchen

Nothing left

I was told to get down to Stony Stratford, get some screens and models and talk for half an hour to the Women's Institute about what the Agora in Wolverton was. There were all these ladies in chairs, arranged in semicircles – must have been 100, 200 – and they all knitted. Every one of them. They didn't look up once. I finished the talk and they put their knitting needles down and they set about me. Why hadn't we got bus services? Why hadn't we got this? I was just a token target – I was pinned against the wall. I said, 'We'll get somebody to contact you on that, but really I'm just here to talk about the development'. And they kept going. This was classic Wolverton – there was nothing left of me, just a pool of sweat really. Then this woman closed the meeting and they presented me with a biro. Then they cleared the table and had a bring-and-buy sale. And we were made to go and spend money in front of witnesses.

Wayland Tunley

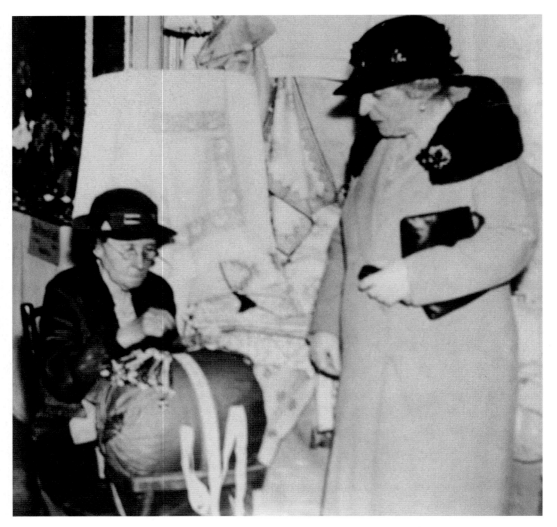

The Princess Royal observing Mrs Wootton of Creed Street, Wolverton, lacemaking at the Great Exhibition, 1920s.

five

Wartime and
Hard Times

Fenny Stratford Home Guard: Shooting contest outside the
Bletchley Park pavilion, 1944.

Sending off recruits at Wolverton, 1914.

Private Arthur Lewis Lloyd, RAMC 61048

I have known Arthur Lewis Lloyd all his life. He passed through this school successfully, being top boy. This last year he has been a student teacher and has shown himself to be a patient and painstaking teacher, conscientious in the discharge of his duties and exemplary in conduct. He is also a capable musician, a good swimmer and plays other games with considerable ability.

H.J. Hippsley, Headmaster,
Wolverton Boys' School, 1914

The following are all letters from Arthur Lewis Lloyd

June 1915, Isleworth

Dear Mother,
I have given my name to join the Army at the end of this term. I expect you will be much upset, but I will obtain what I came to College for, the [Teaching] Certificate. I have not rushed into it. It's practically a year now since the war commenced and I've thought about it ever since. We are not doing at all well either. I feel a lot easier now I've decided to join.

Your loving son, Lewis

July 1915, Aldershot

Dear Mother,
We arrived here today. We had gloves, a body belt and a vest issued to us as special kit so we won't hurt for a bit. We are ten to a tent, sleeping on boards with three blankets, no mattress or pillow. We use our mess tins now. I think we are going to France soon. Of course we know nothing. At any rate, France on the whole is the best of fighting areas.

Your loving son, Lewis

October 1915, France

Dear Mother,

I told you we came over in my last letter. I am quartered in a barn. We have straw for beds. Also I have a waterproof sheet to lie on. Besides an overcoat, I have a rubber mackintosh. I'm quite all right.

Your affectionate son, Lewis

December 1915

Dear Mother,

As I must put no military news in this letter, all I will say is that I have been about 200 yards off the nearest shells. I am now practically free of vermin. I'm still continuing in good health. The weather out here is very changeable though. Last weekend there was a very hard frost. This weekend there is rain and it's very mild. There is a great deal of mud, and boots and puttees and trousers get covered with it. This is the dressing station from which the patients are sent down to the ambulance hospital. We live in the cellar of a brewery – itself in ruins, but the cellars are fairly intact. We have palliasses on stretchers for beds and very comfortable they are.

Your affectionate son, Lewis

January 1916

Dear Mother,

I have not been able to write since Saturday as I was thrown out of a lumber wagon and skinned my hands. I'm all right now. Before I was too busy. Put some candles in the next parcel.

With love, Lewis

May 1916

Dear Mother,

I received your letter yesterday. I am quite well. I am up the line again. The weather conditions are much better now, though it gets warm at times. We have been bombed heavily today and yesterday. Yesterday we had tear gas over. It makes one's eyes smart. I am stretcher-bearing with the ambulance now. We have not had a rest lately.

Your affectionate son, Lewis

June 1916

Dear Mother,

I am quite well. I hope you are all well. We found a stray dog ratting yesterday so we joined in. It disturbed two large ones, one of which it killed, then it got at the nest and killed the young ones. We would have taken it in hand but the sergeant ordered the contrary and we were forced to drive it away. There are some huge rats here, there's always mice where we go.

Your affectionate son, Lewis

July 1916

Dear Mother,

I am quite well. The weather is changeable. I received your letter and Percy's card last week. I've had no time to write. I can say no more but am sending this to let you know I am safe so far.

Your affectionate son, Lewis

August 1916

Dear Mr Lloyd,

It is with deepest regret that I have to inform you of the death in action of your son 61048 Pte A.L. Lloyd on the 20th inst. A shell came into the dugout where he was sitting and injured him so severely that he died half an hour later. He became unconscious almost at once so that at least you have the poor comfort of knowing that his death was practically painless. The shell was a gas shell. You can at least have the satisfaction of knowing that your son was not a conscientious objector and that he died as a man should die!

I am, yours faithfully,

Anderson Meaden, Lieut.Col., RAMC OC
141st Field Ambulance

Wolverton Boys School with headmaster Harry Hipsley, 1897.

England is done for

A little boy, nine years old, was, at Stony Stratford Sessions, given six strokes of the birch rod for stealing a 10s note and some stamps from Mr A. Allen, bootmaker, in whose service he was employed. It appears the boy spent the money on chocolates and a flashlight. The darkness was responsible for the flashlight for, being an errand boy who was obliged to attend school, he could not see the numbers of the houses in the evening when the master sent him out with parcels. What straits employers must be in for labour, when it is necessary to impress a mere baby for the delivery of boots! This must not be seen by the censor, for if reported by wireless it may encourage the Germans to think England is done for.

The *Bucks Advertiser and Aylesbury News*,
1 January 1916

Buried like a rabbit

Well, I'm sitting down, buried like a rabbit, not as deep as I should like to be under the conditions, but you can take my word for it, I'm deep enough to be safe from the Little Snipers. They do not worry us to a great extent. It is the coalboxes or Jack Johnsons that worry us. It is bad enough to hear them screaming over us through the air, but it is like being in hell to get them bursting in front or anywhere near us. The terrific noise, shake, smoke and the waiting for them to drop as one hears them coming is a thing I cannot explain. It is awful waiting to hear and feel the explosion so as to be able to breathe once again freely and wait for the scream of the next one. They leave a hole large enough to bury a horse. Never did I dream of the different sort of things done by the European race that has been done here. The hundreds of thousands of homes in Belgium and France that have been purposely robbed and ruined is a disgrace to any nation. It is an awful sad sight to see as we came through the villages and towns, but what in heaven's name must have been in the thoughts of the French Tommy? Germans were left strewn all up the roads and in the hedges, also the woods. Some were ghastly. It is really a game of luck and we shall be glad to be out of it. There's no doubt our boys are in wonderful good spirit. Perhaps you may be sitting in the trenches holding a mothers' meeting, when all of a sudden one of our big guns may fire from right behind us – it is sport to see us all bob down. But only let me scrape through safely and I shall always think of all the boys and their splendid spirit.

When we have had the chance to buy a loaf of bread out here, we have had to pay as much as ½d. Still, I expect we must not grumble.

Letter dated 30 October 1914 from either Jim or Jack Stallard, of Bradwell parish, who joined the 2nd Expeditionary Force. Both brothers were killed in November 1914

Sitting like waterbirds

Newport and Olney sit like waterbirds in their nests, surrounded by raging floods and the water is rising in the lower streets of each town.

The Bucks Advertiser and Aylesbury News, 4 March 1916

That's cowardice

After the war, when I came back to Wolverton to work, I was a bodymaker. Each of those ambulance coaches, we had to strip out the whole interior and turn them into brake vans. Every one had got a padded cell to put men in that had collapsed in the trenches. There was such a hell of an outcry in England when it became realised what was happening, so many people having to face firing squads, that the British Headquarters altered their tune completely and called it shell shock. They put these padded cells in and they was brought back over to England. Your local paper would have the headlines, 'Local lad, well-known athlete Bill Brown, his mother had a lovely letter from the colonel – "died in action fighting for his country"' – that rubbish was put in the paper and yet the poor bugger had been stuck up against a wall and shot for cowardice. I've been like it meself. We've all been like it at times in the trenches. One day it don't affect you a little bit – you feel a treat. They're shelling and messing about firing, but you don't seem to worry. Another day you just feel the opposite, a bit jittery, and think, 'Ooh hell, I wish they'd pack it in, stop it'. You've got that feeling though, you can't help it, and if you happen to have one of them turns and anything goes wrong, that's cowardice again, you can't help it.

Hawtin Mundy

Rough and cheap-looking

The Stony Stratford Rangers ran a number of jumble sales during the war. The women who came to buy would push the door in, each trying to get in first. And whilst they kept us, the stallholders, occupied pricing an item, their children would be below the level of the stall, filling their bags for free. It was not civilized as sales are today, and the clothes for sale were rough and cheap-looking – much was only suitable for the ragman.

Audrey Lambert

The Land Army

They did everything: hedge-cutting, ditching, tractor-driving – you name it, they done it. Some was living in Woolstone and some at the farm. I got on all right with them. Ruth Kemp, the first Land Army girl I had, come

A sit in at the Wolverton Works in 1925, just before the 1926 General Strike.

from Stratford, a nice person. Then there was Dicky Bird, a tractor driver. They were all fun, they were.

Joseph Willis

Working at Bletchley Park (BP)

I worked at BP during the war, cleaning. You weren't allowed in a room without an escort. You'd spread sawdust mixed with paraffin on the floor – it looked lovely. I was there on D-Day – it was ever so exciting. We weren't even allowed to pick up waste paper. I worked mainly in RAF rooms – the map room, the typing room – but you didn't look at anything. I was vetted when I applied for the job.

Winifred Ottery

Perpetual jet lag

I arrived at BP, or Station X as it was called, in spring 1942. Like nearly everyone else, we worked three shifts, changing every week. It gave us all perpetual jet lag.

Ruth Ross

Possibly shot

Like so many other workers at BP, I had only a small idea of what anyone else did, as we had all been sworn to secrecy and never discussed our work even with each other. Someone gave all the new intake a pep talk when we first arrived and told us bluntly that if we talked about our work we would be court-martialled and possibly shot!

Rozanne Colchester

Brilliant brains

I worked in Hut 7 and was involved in deciphering Japanese naval codes. I had to learn around 1,000 different Japanese characters. Nine of us out of 500 were picked to work for Bletchley Park. I had an aptitude for maths, which helped. There were some brilliant brains – men who could do *The Times* crossword without writing in a single clue. They could visualize the answers in their head.

Ruth Roberts

All hell let loose

On night shift when the German codes hadn't been broken, we could nod off but once the codes were broken, it was all hell let loose. We were allowed to knit, sew when there wasn't very much going on.

Hilary Powell

They disappeared

Secrecy was so ingrained in me that for thirty years I didn't even tell my husband. If he asked what I did in the war, I just said it was something to do with radio and changed the subject. Anyone caught discussing their work disappeared. They were arrested and gone within minutes. Miss S, a

philology lecturer at King's [College], was apparently going to parties in London and bragging about what she was doing. I don't know what they did with her.

Marie Bennett

Christmas Day, 1944

My group worked on the evening of Christmas Day, 1944. We had a very small Christmas tree, which the day shift had left, and we hung our gifts on it – razor blades for each of the men, and they bought us cords of Kirby hairgrips – very welcome, as they were in great demand to keep our longer hair above our jacket collars at the back. We also exchanged writing paper, envelopes, stamps and pen nibs.

G.E. Sweetland

Awful lot of boils

Because I had done a bit of training at Guy's Hospital, I helped out in the sick bay at BP.

Putting up blackout screens in the Wolverton Works body shop, 1939.

There seemed to be an awful lot of boils and I had to bathe these wretched things. Looking back now, I think they were caused by malnutrition. The sick bay was just across from the lake, on a little hill. I used to give first-aid lectures during the lunch hour, in a hut outside the main building where they also used to sell beer. A few people from the huts used to come but you never knew their names or where they actually came from; they were amorphous.

Sheila Lancaster

Our own mortuary
At BP, we had our own mortuary, hospital and fire brigade.

Hilary Powell

In a frightful state
In winter, when it was blackout from about five o'clock, the stench from BP's canteen was quite appalling. Our billet was wet: we got wood from a woodyard, lit a fire in the room and got ticked off about it. Corporal W went home on leave and left a bar of chocolate in her tin hat. When she got back, it had been eaten by the mice! F was a medical orderly in our room, who wheezed and snored all night. When I had pleurisy, I couldn't lie down because it was extremely painful. The doctor said I should be sitting up instead of lying down. It was interpreted that I should be getting up and therefore going back to work. I remember going to work for the evening shift in pouring rain. I was in a frightful state.

Joyce Rushworth

Winston Churchill
A lot of people were billeted in Bletchley. The childless couple next door had WAAFs from Bletchley Park. We knew Winston Churchill came to Bletchley Park by train. He came through the spinney between the station and the Park, but it was all top secret.

Meg Bates

Great excitement
There was great excitement when Churchill came to see us and stood talking to us all and thanking us for our efforts.

Olive E. Keppel-Powis

Nobody knew anything
Nobody knew anything about Bletchley Park. We had a WAAF billeted with us – a linguist, spoke four languages – then a civil servant who shuffled paper. Townspeople knew they were clever people there but nothing else. My cousin worked in there but never said what she was doing. She'd been sending messages to her husband but didn't know it was him. I knew somebody in army signals who sent messages to Bletchley Park. Tabs were kept on her for years.

Roy Maycock

Her ways didn't fit
We had a girl from Bletchley Park. Her mother was on speaking terms with the Queen Mother. Her ways didn't always fit. When she lived here, she wore a pair of old trousers and a shooting jacket, but when she went to London to visits Dukes and so on, she wore a fur coat and real pearls. Bletchley Park people always called Bletchley 'the village'. This annoyed the locals.

Eileen Cordon

Ode to Bletchley Park

I think that I shall never see,
A sight as curious as BP.
This place called up at war's behest,
And peopled with the queerly dressed.
Yet what they did they could not say,
Nor ever shall till Judgment Day.

For six long years have we been there,
Subject to local scorn and stare.
We came by transport and by train,
The dull, the brilliantly insane.
What were we for? Where shall we be
When God at last redunds BP?

If I should die think this of me –
I served my country at BP.
And should my son ask, What did you,
In the Atomic World War Two?
God only knows, and He won't tell,
For after all, BP is HELL!

Anne Ross

The devil

During the war, four Italians – 'collaborators' – worked with us on the farm. They were good blokes, lived in a cottage along Watling Street. Then, at potato-picking time, we had fascists from Haversham – there was a camp there. They made out they didn't understand what you said to them, but they knew all along. While Lucket [the farmer] was there, he'd stand on the back of the tractor, smoke his pipe and he'd be watching them – they'd work like the devil. But when he weren't there, I was in charge and I couldn't get them to work so well. One of them came to me one day and said, 'Lavatory all right?' He went at ten o'clock and didn't come back till twelve. We got rid of him then, the devil.

Joseph Willis

A nasty old job

I got my call-up papers at the end of the war, four days after my eighteenth birthday. My first posting was in Hamelin – carting off bodies of war criminals from the jail. They were hanged three at a time. We had a convoy of Bedford trucks. We took the bodies up onto a mountain in a mass unmarked grave. They weren't allowed flowers, it was just a hole – bomp! – and that was it. It was said to be the mountain where the Pied Piper of Hamelin took the children. Three would be hanged, lassoed, pulled up, the lasso would be taken off and they would be lowered down to the man downstairs, who would remove the shoes and sling them into a corner. Then the bodies would be buried in whatever they had been hanged in. There were a couple of nails in the coffin. I and the other drivers were not allowed in while the hanging was taking place. We just went in afterwards and took the bodies out. There were about eighty a day being hanged – £15 per man and £25 per woman. Women had to be strapped up. I was told that when they are hanged the stomach virtually falls through the womb. I worked on this for three days – I don't know how many were hanged. It was a nasty old job, but it had to be done and that was it.

Frank Bodimead

Too hard

I was born in Sicily in 1934 and came to England in 1954, to work at Bletchley brickworks. I lived in a hostel with many Italians. I wanted to go back home again because the food was not nice, always potato soup. We were not allowed to cook for ourselves. I was at the brickworks for four years, but it was too hard. I had to draw bricks out of the moulding place, put them on barrels and take them to the lorries. The more bricks we carried the more money we got. They were very hot. By the time it was Wednesday or Thursday, you could not touch them.

Francesco Russo

A terrible thing

In 1967, we had the foot-and-mouth outbreak, a terrible thing. Our market was shut for a time. Thousands of cattle were slaughtered. It got as close as Houghton. It really was a scare. We thought we had marvellous compensation for the cattle market [from MKDC] but by 1979 it was worth bugger all with inflation. Old Harold Wilson kept saying, 'It does not alter the pound in your pocket', but of course it jolly well did. We got to over 20 per cent per annum.

Dicky Arnold

Heaven costs

There was a lot of Habitat furniture [in the show houses] – slightly upmarket. It was unfortunate that they hadn't put second-hand furniture in, to make it look a bit more ordinary. After all, some people coming from the East End didn't have any money at all, but Milton Keynes was their heaven and it was going to be just perfect. They were sorely disappointed when they found out how much it would cost them.

June Whittaker

Treated violently

We were aware there might be women who were being treated violently in their homes. We'd go round and talk to the Lions Clubs, Rotary Clubs, Round Tables, magistrates, Housewives' Registers, Women's Institutes. We pooled about twenty people who expressed an interest and formed the Milton Keynes Women's Aid. The problem was, women didn't leave an address if they'd left home. If they stayed at home, they were at risk. So we had to have somewhere they could stay. Eventually, we were given a farmhouse.

Carole Loxton

Helpless

A widow, Mary Ann Barley, seventy-six years of age, was fined five shillings for having been helplessly drunk in Market Place, Stony Stratford, she having, in her own words, indulged in 'two penn'orth of whisky'.

The *Bucks Advertiser and Aylesbury News*,
8 January 1916

The Royal Bucks Yeomanry marching in Bletchley Road, 1939.

six

New City
Development

The 'largest steam tram in the world' that ran between Stony Stratford and Wolverton for forty years, from 1886-1926.

Something special

Milton Keynes has somehow defied the laws of gravity in this country over the last two decades. When things have been going down in somewhat of a long sliding decline, Milton Keynes has somehow been putting things up – buildings, trees, businesses, spirits. There's something special that has been happening here.

Sir Peter Parker at the opening of the new DRS company headquarters at Linford Wood, September 1985

Second to none

You can't stop progress. The city had to come. What they have done with flowers, trees and gardens to stop the city looking like a concrete jungle is wonderful. It's second to none.

Ernie and Muriel Smith

A good place to locate, 1859

Wolverton is 52½ miles from London and 59¾ miles from Birmingham, a good place to locate the Grand Central Depot of the London-Birmingham Railway. This station is an extensive establishment and will probably give rise to the formation of a new town. Upwards of fifty cottages belonging to the servants of the company have already sprung into existence.

Osbourne's Railway Guide of 1859

Nine days' wonder, 1944

In the middle of the war, the Abercrombie Report came out. To our great excitement, it named Bletchley as a suggested site for a new town. I went up to London for a press conference and the *Bletchley Gazette*, of which I was editor, really 'splashed' it but Abercrombie proved to be a nine days' wonder. The experts ruled that Bletchley couldn't expand because of the inability to provide satisfactory sewage disposal and water supply. The locals were greatly disappointed.

Ron Staniford

Burnt on my heart

The new town of Milton Keynes was designated on 17 January 1967, a famous date that everyone's forgotten, but it's burnt on my heart because I had to act for all those farmers who lost their land. The sensible ones immediately bought land outside the area. Some retired. Many were caught up by inflation: when they came to buy, the value of farmland had gone up and they didn't get as many acres for the compensation they got, which seemed very unfair to us. The new city acquired the land and they would allow you to continue farming for a few years as a licensee, but most farmers said 'bother it' and cleared off.

Dicky Arnold

I hated it

I was sixty when Milton Keynes was taking over. I hated it. I did all I could to stop it. The prices weren't good, but we had to take what we could get.

Lol King

Grandiose plans

I first found out about the new city with the Chamber of Trade: we invited Fred Pooley, the architect from Aylesbury, to address the Chamber on what the coming of a 'new town' would be. He had grandiose plans for a new city with a monorail – known as 'Pooleyville', a very imaginative scheme. The monorail would travel all round the periphery, the centre reserved for a park-like area, and all the facilities around the outskirts with no congestion in the centre – very innovative.

Brian Barnes

I liked things new

I first heard of the new city plan at middle school in Bletchley, that Bletchley, Stony Stratford and Wolverton would be its corner-stones. It was very exciting. Teachers took opportunities to talk about what a new city entailed. They were excited too, with career opportunities, something new and fresh, everyone working together from the same starting block, learning as announcements were made. I was very enthusiastic. I liked things new. I was a fan of the Thunderbirds and liked the futuristic vision of the new city, centred round a monorail!

Peter Truscott

First to be uprooted

In 1967, the news of the city came to us fairly sudden. All the farmers tried to stop it and push it over onto someone else, but we weren't very successful. It came bit by bit. It was a hor-rible feeling. We were one of the first to be uprooted. They put a north-south road right through the middle of my farm in 1970/71. It was all compulsorily purchased and I rented it back until they developed it. They started putting in mains drains and you couldn't get cattle from one field to another or into the buildings and into the yard, so they had to go.

Tony King

Beautifully drawn

The Master Plan for Milton Keynes had been done before the Corporation was set up. It said where the main housing areas would be, where the employment was, and the city centre and so on. And of course, it set out the grid road struc-ture. Each part of the city district – two or three grid squares – was designed in detail by a team of people and that had to be approved by the EMC, [Executive Management Committee] –

the equivalent of a board of a private company with the powers of a planning committee. You realize now how much effort went into those designs. They actually thought about where the buildings were going, how they would relate to each other and how the landscape infrastructure would relate – very important in Milton Keynes. The process involved a multidiscipli-nary team of landscape architects, quantity sur-veyors to assess costs, structural and civil engineers, architects and town planners. The illustrations were quite beautifully drawn.

Peter Bowtell

Piping in the visitors to a new building in the city centre, 1981. MKDC General Manager Frank Henshaw (1980-1993) is fifth in line behind piper Donald Reid of the Milton Keynes Pipe Band.

Simpson village before development, c. 1970.

Very, very quick

The Estates side [of MKDC] had to get the land to start with, but the Engineering side had to get in at day one – to organize aerial surveys and look after all the contact with the gas, water, electricity. We had British Waterways, the River Authority, the main line rail line and the trunk road going right through the middle of the place. So a lot of discussions went on separately from the Master Plan – on drainage and highways – because the trouble was, the statutory authorities never realised how big it was. We were planning for 240,000 people and we had to do it very, very quick – 150,000 in the first ten years. They'd never faced anything of that size from scratch. Earlier rounds of new towns were 60-90,000. Then they brought in the big ones at Peterborough and Northampton – but they were based on existing county boroughs. Milton Keynes was the only one of its size to be based on open land from about 40,000 people.

Ernest Pye

So excited

When I first joined the Corporation, you went to work by coach because the road system was non-existent. On my coach were architects from all over the world – Americans, Japanese and Germans. They were so excited to be working on a completely new development.

Janice Walker

The whole man

A proper architect is the whole man. It's from the ground upwards. It's from the environment, it's everything. It's not just a person who designs buildings. An architect deals with the whole of the environment and people's aspirations in that environment. Now there are very few people like that around. An architect today is one of two people. He's either a hack who can knock out a building for a developer that will pass a planning committee and will stand up and will be about the right price, or he's some higher being who designs a very beautiful building which is a wonderful concept but which has major flaws, like it leaks or it's three times over budget.

David Stabler

Wacky ideas

I was group secretary to the architects' department at MKDC, a very exciting place because we had quite a lot of architects with wacky ideas like strange colours – brown, red and yellow factories! We had this period when every thing seemed to be yellow – a prototype factory was built on the lawn at Wavendon Tower. The screens between the desks had to be yellow, the desks were yellow, the carpet was yellow. Everything was yellow. It must have affected me because I actually painted our bedroom at home brown.

Ceiling, walls – all chocolate brown. Very womb–like and you couldn't see a thing. But that was the result of having worked with these guys. It was great fun. Fantastically exciting. It was a wonderful job. I didn't realise how lucky I was to be working there. Everybody was so enthusiastic.

Sue Malleson

Children knew more

Planners used to go into the schools with plans and models. So the children knew more about the changes taking place than their parents.

Marion Fox

Tongue-tied

My wife had persuaded me to give a talk to her sixth-formers about the new city of Milton Keynes. I stood up on the stage with the plan of Milton Keynes and the slide show and I was rabbiting on and got to education and secondary schools. I said, 'And of course all our schools are going to be…' – the word I was trying to recall was 'co-educational', but I couldn't pull it up and I said – '…bisexual!' We promised each other we'd never perform on stage together again.

Bob Hill

It really dawned

I remember doing Milton Keynes in geography in the sixties – the teacher wrote it on the blackboard and drew the designated area. It didn't really bother me at the time as a teenager or anyone I knew. It sort of crept up slowly. It was only when I went to visit some of the new estates that it really dawned. I thought some of the new houses were really weird. When I first married, we lived in New

Early city infrastructure development (roads and sewers), 1972.

Bradwell. There were cows at the bottom of the garden. They used to stick their heads through the hedge. Then the cows disappeared and they started blasting for the sewerage works for Bradville and Stantonbury. But you just accepted it.

Zena Flinn

It never stopped

They were always building, right from when we were here [Bletchley]. The motorway went up, the Saints estate went up, then Whaddon Way. It never stopped. Then the new city came. Look at the size of it now!

Ronald Flinn

Biggest and best

I've had a passion for new towns and for the opportunities they gave people of all kinds to get interesting work and not be choked by the systems and the politics – the worst aspects of this country. So I was immediately attracted to Milton Keynes, the biggest and best new town.

Neil Higson

The Battle of Little Big Horn

We did presentations [to company employees] about them moving with their company to Milton Keynes. We had people from Social Development, from Housing, and people like

Geoff Cooksey, before he even had Stantonbury Campus, so there was an educational point. You'd stand at the back of the room, where sixty or seventy employees with their husbands or wives had been invited for the evening, and the Managing Director would stand up and say, 'I've got some really super news for you. We're closing down our branch here and we're thinking of relocating to Milton Keynes. Oh, and by the way, I've got somebody at the back who's going to talk to you about Milton Keynes.' And you would duck, because then it was like the Battle of Little Big Horn. Out came the bows and arrows and you had to take the flak. We were there to say, 'Look – we're not justifying why your company wants to move to Milton Keynes. We're here to tell you what Milton Keynes is, what it's all about, how it all hangs together.'

Rodney Markley

A family feel

It was a very creative environment and you just got on with it. The best thing was being able to go out and help folk get settled into a new community – the excitement of it all. There was this great motivation and commitment and there was a sort of family feel to it, even though it was a big organization.

Ruth Salter

We need the jobs

A company would come in and we'd sit around and comment on their designs. The Corporation had quite a lot of power when you think how they convinced quite large companies to make major changes to the design of their buildings. There was sometimes some friction with the Estates Department in the Corporation, who were obviously anxious to get these companies here. They'd say, 'You mustn't frighten them off. We need them here, we need the jobs.' So it was a very fine balancing act trying to get an acceptable design and keeping the company comfortable with coming to Milton Keynes. Sometimes, threats were made: 'If we get messed around any more, we're not coming!'

Peter Bowtell

Deep drainage

I worked for a firm called Streeters, which did most of the underground tunnelling for Milton Keynes – the deep drainage. We went down at seven o'clock in the morning, not coming out until ten o'clock at night, from underground. I was actually lining them up because, digging underground, they couldn't see where they were going. You had to put in string lines so they could dig in a straight line. There were generators with lights underground and they had trains too with little carriages. They'd dig the clay out and put it in the carriages, then run back to the manhole shafts. Cranes used to lift the soil out – there were big heaps where they'd been digging the tunnels. Most of the miners lived on site and then go home to Birmingham or London for the weekend. But they were earning fantastic money – £250 a week, about £1,000 nowadays, I should think.

Brian O'Sullivan

The Wolverton Bath House, 1889

As Mr Webb has now got the new pumping station south of the Blue Bridge here at work, and is desirous of removing the old pumping engine and converting the Green Lane tank house (where the only baths in Wolverton are situated) into cottages, I shall be glad if your committee will authorise me to erect baths in the space between the finishing and repairs

Lord Campbell of Eskan, first MKDC Chairman 1967-1983 (back row, second from left) at City Centre Library with the winners of a 'New City' poster competition and fellow judges, 1982.

shops on the Stratford Road as shown in a plan, which I will submit at an estimated cost of £500.

Letter of 8 November 1889, submitted to the Locomotive Committee at Euston about the Bath House at Wolverton, now the base for the Living Archive.

Clean enough for fish

The water seems much cleaner now, with the city. We used to get a lot of pollution from an ink factory at Mount Farm. You could literally see the water marks under the sheep's chins – well, generations of animals drank from the river and it wasn't until we started getting pollution from the factories they put water troughs in for us. It's only since the city that the river, especially in the Woolstone area, has been clean enough for fish.

Sam Sinfield

No flooding now

At one time you couldn't get from Simpson to Walton because the River Ouzel used to flood there very, very often. The field flooded as well – always flooded until the Development Corporation built the balancing lake. I can't recall anywhere in Milton Keynes flooding now.

Kenneth Page

Balancing lake – for flood prevention and as a leisure amenity – under construction, 1972.

Willen Lake finds

We found a mammoth's tusk when we were constructing Willen Lake, and a vertebrae of a fish called a plectasaurus, about thirty foot long. I gave that to Bradwell Abbey Museum.

Brian O'Sullivan

Quick effect

If you want to have an impact rather than a tree mix which will be slow to develop but be wonderful in thirty years, then you look into the techniques of using semi-mature trees for a very quick effect.

Neil Higson

Catastrophic

Speed and confidence were vital. In the early days, Milton Keynes was taking one hell of a lot of stick and investor confidence was wanting. It took a huge leap of the imagination to actually visualize what this place would look like. The trees were tiny; the roads were vast. It was difficult to see how this would ever become the City of Trees. It wasn't helped by the two droughts. 1975 was bad and '76 was horrendous – there's a *Daily Mail* centre spread of me with just dead trees, little saplings all wilted and dead. That was catastrophic.

Brian Salter

Willen Lake filling up, mid-1970s.

Bending and stooping

I worked for thirteen years doing landscaping for MKDC, planting trees and shrubs. They had to be planted to a certain standard and inspected. Everything was set in a grid pattern – whichever way you looked, everything was in line, in theory. The first few days at the tree nursery I found a bit hard because all the time we were pulling out and bundling small plants – a lot of bending and stooping. Most of the first week, I was ready for a bath and bed. Then I began to get into the swing of things – of course they all took the mick out of me, calling me 'lilly-white hands'. Three weeks later, my hands were all callused and scraped and they said, 'That's more like it!' We had to plant up the island at Willen Lake. At great expense, the Corporation hired a helicopter, which flew trees and materials to the island. We'd row ourselves across in a boat and were there for the day. We had to rig ourselves up some shelter because it was appalling weather – we were out there digging tree pits. All the trees survived, surprisingly.

Peter Bunnage

Strings, beads and settings

One of the main things I did in bringing landscape architects into one team was to get them to really believe in themselves and their subject, making places for people to have decent lives in. It's terrific when people actually like the product and it's contributing to their quality of life. The most important thing we did was the linear park system, devising the principle of 'strings, beads and settings' – so there were public routes and footpaths; planted areas, pony paddocks, sports fields, university areas; and there was the Camphill Trust farm and the Japanese school, pubs and sports centres – 'beads' of activities.

Neil Higson

A little green space

The greatest success for me is that there's more greenery and plants in Milton Keynes than concrete and bricks. If you stand in the city centre and look at V8 [Marlborough Street] and round the top of Campbell Park – that's the bit that impresses me the most.Even today when you walk a grid square, you find a little green space that you didn't know was there and a load of trees. Lovely! I wouldn't change it.

Jeff Fawcett

Twenty million units

Over twenty million 'units' – shrubs, trees and bulbs – were planted in Milton Keynes.

Brian Salter

Four bricks

It was about 1978 when MKDC arranged to take people to where the new shopping centre was going to be built. It was a field with four bricks at one end and four at the other.

Marion Fox

Enormous building site,1979

I was driving for ready-mixed concrete when we worked on the city centre, pouring in all the bases. It was an enormous building site. You couldn't tell what it was. It was just poles and holes, thirty foot square, with signs saying, 'This is hole one', 'This is hole two' etc. We were putting in the bases for the

New planting in the Ouse Valley, Milton Keynes Linear Park, 1979.

Central Milton Keynes being built, c. 1979.

steelwork – thirty foot cubes of concrete. Massive – that's the size of a house. I'd back up to a hole, pour a great load of concrete down the hole and say, 'There you go', and another lorry would be pushing you out the way to put his load in. They'd put six or seven lorryloads straight into one hole. And that was the base for the steelwork. They said the bases for the concrete are designed to last 5,000 years. When it first opened and we saw it, it was wonderful – wow, what a size this place was! It was the largest shopping centre in Europe, each mall down each side half-a-mile long!

David Webb

Extent of the building so great, 1859

The engine house of Wolverton Works is of quadrangular form, each side being 314 feet long. It is built of brick with stone cornice and blockings, the style of the architecture being Doric. The extent of the building is so great that it has a very imposing appearance. Also being erected are shops for engines, tender sheds, join- ers' shop, iron foundry, boiler yard, hooping furnaces, iron warehouse, smithy, turning shops, offices, stores, a steam engine for giving motion to the machinery and for pumping water into a large tank over the entrance gateway to supply the locomotive engines and an area of two acres set aside for a wharf adjacent to the canal, and waiting and refreshment rooms.

Osbourne's Railway Guide of 1859

Indoors for the big shops

Some people called the shopping centre in the city centre a white elephant when it first opened but I recall the slogan for CMK: 'Shopping as it should be'. I believe that to be true even twenty years on, having had the experience of not having to worry about the weather when going to the shops. The big attraction of MK is that it is exclusively indoors for the big shops.

Peter Truscott

Part of my success

At first I did not like the coming of Milton Keynes very much. I felt the rural area of Bucks had been destroyed and I did love the villages around, they were lovely. But as time went by and the roads were built, the shopping centre came along, the factories and offices were being built – it brought a lot of work into the area and for that I am glad for MK development. As a businessman in the area for twenty-five years, I think that part of my success is because of MK.

Donato Piselli

Dramatic changes

The building has been colossal here – the businesses that have come into Milton Keynes, the houses that have gone up, the Housing Associations that have come along with different types of houses. The opportunities have changed quite a lot because, as you've lived here for so many years, you've changed – you've progressed and you've had a bit of time to save some money so you can be a bit more choosy. So it's been quite dramatic changes that I've seen – the hospital, the city centre shops. It's a really good place.

Kathy Sellick

Harvest Festival Service in the Central Milton Keynes Shopping Building, 1979.

The dome being placed on the City Church, 1990.

seven

Country Folk and City Slickers

Hawtin Mundy (1894-1983), resident of Thompson Street, New Bradwell, whose irrepressible story-telling – of the Great War and of life back home – inspired Living Archive's musical documentary drama 'Days of Pride' and his book, *No Heroes No Cowards*.

Citizen from the start

I had private misgivings about moving to Milton Keynes, but I was determined not to let that show. As the months went by, increasingly I felt that I was more at home here in Milton Keynes than I'd ever been in Oxford. Oxford's a bit like an occupied city – overrun by either students or tourists. I was born there but you feel, if you don't belong to the academic world, you're an outsider. The great thing about coming to Milton Keynes was that one felt like a citizen from the start. Everything was done to encourage people who wanted to make a life for themselves.

William Slee

Advertisement for Milton Keynes, published by MKDC on 1 April 1982.

Ferreting and snaring

I used to catch rabbits and moles – ferreting and snaring, anything that you could catch 'em with. In one week in Howe Park, I caught 600 rabbits – ninepence for every two. That was a good wage that was. I had three ferrets, a male and two females. When you're ferreting, you put the female in the rabbit burrow with a string muzzle on her, so she can't bite the rabbit but can move her jaws. Then she'd bolt the rabbits into nets over the holes. I'd carry about twenty nets. Or she'd push them into a cul-de-sac in the burrow. If she did that, you'd put the male in on a line so that he could tell you – take the line with him. Then you could dig up the line to him. Obviously, when the male came to the rabbit, the female came back out of the burrow. You'd pick her up and put her in the box. I also caught moles with a barrel trap – a wire that traps the mole round the waist.

Bernard Groom

No shooting, more foxes

In the old days, farmers would carry a gun around with them. Any vermin would be shot. You're not supposed to do any shooting now in Milton Keynes. I think there are more foxes because there's no hunting any more. The hunt used to meet in [Woughton] village and come across our land. There was a fox cover up the Bleak Hall area. The foxes now are quite tame. They live in hedgerows. We've had cubs born under the hay in the shed at the bottom of our yard. They feed from people's dustbins. If you had lambs born out in the field, they'd have them.

Tony King

Ploughing with horses

I used to go ploughing with me Dad – start in the morning after breakfast, carry on till three, then put the horses away, give 'em their food, have your dinner, then go out and finish. You'd have two abreast and one in front to lead. I used to ride that in my school holidays, walking up and down, miles. My Dad could set the plough and walk up the side of it – it would go up the field and plough without him holding the handles… We had a bloke spent all day watching him who said he'd never seen a plough go like that before. He was a good ploughman, he were.

Joseph Willis

Sheep are characters

You've got to like sheep to keep sheep 'cos sheep are such a pain in the neck. They've got a habit of either getting out or dying for the slightest thing. Once a sheep gets a problem, it usually dies 'cos there's no resistance, no wish to live. Not with sheep. They've got a death wish from the word go. But I couldn't look at a sheep and say, 'I'll have you for the freezer' – they're lovely characters. In the thick of lambing, you get very little sleep. You can get so edgy when you're tired. You've got to be very fond of them, basically, to keep your cool, 'cos it can be very trying. Sheep are characters.

Sam and Pam Sinfield

Pigs and cattle

We had fifteen pigs, fifteen bullocks in one yard and fifteen in another at Brick Kiln Farm. That was hell to go into the yard there. The pigs would come out, you'd get hold of the pigs and the cattle would come out. What the cattle left, the pigs would eat. They were lovely pigs – hairy Sitworths with patches on. They did get fat. The vet would come and inject them and say, 'We've got to catch the pigs today'. I've never seen blokes like Johnny

and Michael catch pigs in all your life. They got hold of them and was down on the ground quick as lightning, strong as lions though, yeah.

Joseph Willis

That field tells some tales

Where the concrete cows are now was where, when they used to gut all the cattle that had been slaughtered in Wolverton, they used to bring all the no-good innards back there. They'd got pigs in that field and they used to throw it all out to them. That field tells some tales. It was called Muddy Pool. Round Old Bradwell, there was Broads Lay, Watering Pond, Best-Ploughed-Bit, Windmill Bush, Heelands, Manor Farfield, Martin's Meadow, Two-Mile Ash.

George Stevenson

Just to see the lambs

We didn't have cattle because the old Development Corporation didn't like cattle along their parklands because cattle are rather curious – they'll walk after people and frighten them. Our cattle are quiet; they're fussed. You'd often see a husband stood beside one of the animals with his arm touching it, and the wife with a camera. Milton Keynes people love the animals, they do. They love to see a few lambs. When we trough-feed the ewes along the river meadows in the spring, that's a time when the lambs run off and play all over the bank. It's surprising the amount of folk who come along at feed-time, just to see these lambs go.

Sam and Pam Sinfield

Walking into cows

Once I'd left London, I started seeing all the warts there. I'd go to see friends at the weekend

Old Bradwell in 1970, with New Bradwell in the background.

and realized that you've got to plan an hour's journey every time you go to see somebody. The streets were dirty, and although there was lots of things to do, I could still do those and live in Milton Keynes. I'd go back, and people would make jokes about concrete cows and I'd show them photographs of cows within two minutes' walk of my front door. Because you could walk across the road in New Bradwell and be at the side of the river and walking into cows!

Debbie Greaves

Where milk comes from

[When we first moved to Milton Keynes], we'd the canal across the road from us. Christina was three at the time. We were walking along the canal and a cow suddenly sticks its head across the gate, made us all jump a bit. I tried to interest her and said, 'That's where your milk comes from.' She looks round very puzzled and says, 'Well, where's the milk bottles?'

Ken Beeley

Luck money

If you sold animals, the person who bought them would give the person's children money. If Dad sold one, we used to get sixpence as 'luck money'. I don't know whether the luck was for them or for us.

Tony King

He never used to tell us

Farming people tend nowadays to know far more about the scientific side than they ever used to. The vet will talk to us more readily

Willen Lake South, 2002. (courtesy of Milton Keynes Parks Trust)

than he would years ago. Once upon a time, the vet was a sort of equivalent to old gentry. He never used to tell us things.

Sam and Pam Sinfield

All the land that was my farm

Emerson Park Farmhouse was built about 1740. There's a Sun Insurance badge over the door – we've tried to trace the number. It was bought in 1921 by my wife's father, the tenant, from Colonel Selby-Lowndes – he sold it to raise money for death duties. All the land that was my farm is going to be built on. It ran up to Howe Park on the western flank and in a triangle to the Whaddon Road and back to Shenley Brook End. There's part of one field going to be a sports field.

Bernard Groom

A new big back garden

It was just after Christmas we moved here. There was no motorway, just straight down the A5, all in the back of the old removal van, £11. I mean, blimey, that was about three weeks' wages. The house was lovely. We had a big back garden, alleyway between the two houses, three bedrooms.

Ronald Flinn

Glad to leave London

I was glad to leave the cramped conditions in London. We sat in the vegetable lorry and Dad sat in the back. We were very happy with the house but it was hard to get to know people until my son started school. I made friends then.

Betty Clifford

We heard we were moving

I happened to come home from lunch one day – my daughter was playing on the stairs – and there was this meths drinker performing his toiletries down in the cellar area. That made me suddenly say, 'Hold on a minute, we've got to do something about this. It's not an ideal place to bring up children.' The local council office suggested new towns. We heard we were moving to Milton Keynes three weeks after applying!

Ken Beeley

City-slicking brolly

I came up to Milton Keynes on a Friday evening in 1971 for an interview with Alan Ashton [MKDC Chief Estates Officer, 1968-1977]. I'd been sort of 'city-slicking' down in London, so I'd brought my brolly with me, just in case I got wet going from the station to Wavendon Tower.

He thought that was absolutely bloody nonsense: 'You won't want that up here', he said. The thing that struck me was, on the way in to the interview, in reception were two members of staff – Brian Brookman and John Wright. They were still there at seven o'clock on a Friday night. I started talking to them about working at the Corporation and they were just bubbling with enthusiasm. After a five-minute interview, Alan Ashton offered me the job. I suppose I got the feeling that it felt right – I was like a rat up a drainpipe and I joined in January '72.

Bob Hill

It felt like home

I loved Stony Stratford – the people absolutely rallied round remarkably. I remember my husband going into Odell's and it was like Aladdin's cave. He only wanted something like a lock for a door and people said, 'Ooh – are you the new

Mr Kevin Dodds, first tenant of the Central Milton Keynes flats, June 1979.

High Street, Stony Stratford, c. 1900.

people that live at Galley Hill?' We got invited to so many things, it was absolutely amazing – we were very accepted by the old community of Stony Stratford. When we saw the houses, we thought 'Oh my God' because they were mono-pitched roofs but they were really very good houses. It felt like home from day one. I get really angry when people knock Milton Keynes. I think it was the best move we've ever made and I can't think of anywhere better to live.

Norma Loh

That's the order

I moved to the Lakes estate on 13 May 1972 – a very cold Saturday. My wife at the time wanted the hot water put on, she wanted the gas connected, she wanted the heating put on, she wanted the bed doing, all at one go. I sat down on the stairs and said to her, 'Right, I want you to write down everything you want doing, that's the order it's going to be done!'

Ken Beeley

Friends to this day

We got to know our neighbours fairly quickly because we heard a lot of banging going on next door and it was a young couple moving in, putting the central heating in. So I just took a tray of tea in for them and we're still friends to this day.

Kathy Baker

We buy everything

In the beginning, you always think about your friends and your family but gradually you settle down, make your own friends here. Yes, you always think, I had so much money there [Uganda], I had so many things there and we lost everything overnight. When I came [to Wolverton], I worked for the council. I'd do street lighting at night. At weekends, I'd work at Emberton Park and sometimes at the box office at Stantonbury Theatre. Unless you work hard, you are not going to get back to the standard you are used to. We did not want anything for nothing. WRVS women used to come around and say, 'Can we get you this, can we get you that?' I'd say, 'No, we buy everything.'

Ranjeet Toprani

£2 to live on

My basic rate in Richmond in 1972 as a tradesman was £20 a week. A bedsit cost £18 a week! That left you £2 a week to live on. We moved to Milton Keynes and got a house for £7 a week and a basic wage of £26 a week.

Brian O'Sullivan

£2 tree vouchers

Everyone had a £2 tree voucher – they had to be the first in a new house. We became known as the City of Trees. Arrivals workers kept a list of tree vouchers. The tree had to be above a certain height – it couldn't be a shrub. Estates would get together and pool their vouchers, to make a plan for the road. It was a good way to get together. Women did the cooking, children played with buckets and spades, men dug the holes. People got to know each other.

Norma Jamieson and Carole Loxton

Twenty pence for a load

I got to know people on the estate purely because I had children, a dog and several cats. In Great Linford, we were extremely fortunate in having a local centre built and occupied reasonably soon. We had a jolly good Co-op. It had a butcher's and a whole human person standing behind the counter to serve you. It had a greengrocery, a post office and a launderette – which was fantastic for me because I'd still got nappies to do. They had

the most wonderful tumble-dryers – you could do a whole load for about twenty pence.

Sue Burrows

Utterly lost

We suddenly found lorries coming through, utterly lost. They'd say, 'Where's Milton Keynes, mate?' You'd say, 'Well – which bit do you want? Do you want Milton Keynes village?' They'd say, 'Where's that?' You'd say, 'If you take this thundering great artic and go outside the village pub, they won't be very pleased with you'. Especially when we used to play cricket over there.

Henry Dewick

Frost and muck...

A frost in November,
Enough to bear a duck,
All through the winter,
Nothing but mud and muck.

Bernard Groom

...and mud!

The mud! Every house with a porch over it had wellingtons. All the children were trained. Nobody went in anybody's house with their shoes on. They just automatically took them off. My daughter was a bit of a tomboy. She ventured into one square of mud and sank to the tops of her wellies. She stood there calling for help. The workmen were looking out of windows yelling encouragement and one poor boy, only about sixteen, got sent to rescue her. They decided that if they threw a ladder onto the mud and sent him on the ladder, to put his arms under her arms and pull her out, that would do it. It all went well until he got to the end of the ladder. He pulled her out, and

An aerial view of Great Linford local centre under construction, 1975.

she came out of her wellies like a cork out of a bottle and they both went backwards. Ken and I came home and my lovely white walls were spattered with mud – all the way up the stairs, three floors up, and there's this pair of jeans, stiff as a board, standing by the bath where Lynne had got out of them and then gone off to play somewhere else.

June Shrewsbury

They don't understand

Most of the villages are not lived in by country people, they're lived in by commuters. They don't understand the implications of turning a dog out and letting it roam. It starts innocently enough with dogs after rabbits. Then they'll run up and down the hedge and the sheep run and the dogs think it's fun and they give chase. They like it clean too.

Farming is a mucky, dirty job and country folk understand that. I've come across people who haven't got wellies because they don't ever need such things.

Sam and Pam Sinfield

A little while

When you go into a village, it takes a little while for them to take to you.

Ronald Flinn

You could tell the newcomers

I'd meet new residents when I went out for a drink – all sorts. You could tell who were the newcomers. Over time, some became good friends – mainly the older ones. Coming from London, they thought it was a wonderful place – they'd got a house, a job and they're

Early development of the new city in the 1970s. The trunk sewer parts in the background are big enough to drive a car through.

surrounded by all the greenery and the land-scape. I didn't like it because it destroyed my home – the fields were turned into tarmac, the ponds were filled in and estates were built. It is a blot on the landscape. Architects and land-scapers have not improved on nature. They should have left it as it was.

Reginald Booth

Like a dream

We moved to Milton Keynes on 29 August 1975. My first feeling was having an address like Tinkers Bridge sounded a bit like gypsies. But we had a one-bedroom basement flat in London, four of us sleeping in it. It didn't have any bathroom and an outside toilet. When you went to bed at night, you were below ground level so you didn't even have the street lights. You were in complete darkness. The day I moved though, I was really sad. I cracked open a bottle of champagne in this dingy little

flat and I cried. I kept saying, 'I don't know what I'm crying for.' I think it was leaving people and family behind. But this three-bed-roomed house was like a dream – centrally heated, fitted cupboards in the kitchen, the kids had their own bedroom. It was just won-derful, really brilliant. And my Mum and Dad came to live in Milton Keynes twelve years later.

Kathy Sellick

Simple character lost

I have been living in Milton Keynes since 1976. It has been just like watching a baby grow up. When we first arrived, the shopping centre was being built. Before, we went shopping in Bletchley, because the only supermarket in Milton Keynes was there. It was quiet and peaceful. The people were simple and nice. Nowadays, although Milton Keynes is more prosperous, and more Chinese

Old Wolverton in the 1900s.

people settle down here, What a pity the crime rate is rising – it has already lost its simple character. One of my neighbours always harasses me, even though my daughter complained to the police on my behalf. The problem is still hanging over me. This makes me stressed. I live as in hell. I will move to somewhere else in Milton Keynes next year.

Kwan Ying Wong

Our problem

We've had numerous barns built. This was our problem in Milton Keynes. Any barns we've got, full of fodder – hay and straw, very inflammable – was soon burnt out. As soon as the housing estates started to go up, that's when it started, but it's no worse than all over the country as a whole. We've had sheep shot with air guns and killed, and Tony's had cross-bows through them. He saw a piece about three inches sticking out the side of a sheep

and he thought it just went under the skin but, when he pulled it out, it was about a foot long. It obviously must have gone between the entrails, otherwise it would have killed it. And the sheep walked away, it survived. He had about three like it. They were home-made bolts.

Sam and Pam Sinfield

Bombarded by accents

I moved to Britain from Kenya in 1976, when I was eleven. I had grown up with a view of Britain being an idyllic Enid Blyton kind of land, and it was not. It was so far away from that, it was amazing. I came over speaking practically the Queen's English – extremely well, awfully posh, with marbles in my mouth, a bit like Eliza Doolittle. All of a sudden, I was being bombarded by these accents – 'Watcha', 'Oi ya'. That really amazed me.

Soraya Billimoria

Very satisfied

Before I came to Milton Keynes, I read a book called *The Best City*, which is mainly analysis and compared cities in Britain by scoring points. The report included employment, education, crime rate, entertainment. I focused on employment and education. Both had a high score in Milton Keynes. This was why I chose Milton Keynes. I very much enjoy living in Milton Keynes and feel very satisfied with my choice.

Richard Leung

Like a rocket fizzing

When I first came to Inter Action [Peartree Bridge], it was like the rest of Milton Keynes, all bubbling with potential. It was like you open a crack in a door and look into another world. Milton Keynes was like a rocket fizzing before it had taken off. I was fortunate to come just when it lifted off. We were working with adults, children, people with disabilities, volunteers, art groups, anybody who was interested. When most people move, they're in the same boat, getting used to this strange new location. It wasn't like any other town they'd been to – it was all bits and pieces and the grand plan couldn't be seen. There would be the honeymoon period of the new property – get your garden together, children at school, job – and then you start looking round for things to do. We had to put an awful lot of work into capturing the public's imagination: street theatre, photography clubs, firework displays, processions, gardening clubs. The real work comes in reaching people who are shy and feel it's not for them. That takes a tremendous amount of energy. We tried to be all things to everybody.

Tracy Walters

Inter Action Community Arts Group, 1980s.

eight

Communities and Friends

Bletchley Park maids and maintenance workers outside the mansion, 1906.

Danger to those travelling

During the last few weeks, we have been compelled to mention the very unsatisfactory condition of the Wolverton to Stratford road. Statistics amply bear out the justice of our demands. The total tonnage of traffic passing over the Great Bath Road, probably the most used road in the country, in an average of sixteen hours, is 1,400 tons. The traffic passing over the Watling Street for a similar period is 400 tons. On our own Wolverton Road, the day tonnage averages 960 tons. In the face of these figures, the necessity for macadamizing of the road is very obvious. The road is constantly used and, both in the interests of the walking and the travelling public, this innovation should be undertaken with a minimum of delay. The condition of the road during the past winter was a danger to those travelling upon it and such a state of things can hardly be tolerated again.

Wolverton Express, 8 May 1914

Constant procession

I spent my first night in Stony Stratford in what used to be Grainger's Food Stores on the High Street. I was impressed by all the lorries going through on the main road – the main trunk road to London and through to the North in those days. There was a constant procession of lorries going past. I think it was 4 a.m. before I went to sleep.

'NS'

Bop, bop, bop

The Stony Stratford tram depot was in St Mary's Avenue. The tram was drawn by steam engines. It ran from the top of town outside the Foresters to the railway station at Wolverton, where it turned round and came back again. There used to be a stop at King Street. It didn't stop again until the printworks. When it couldn't get up the hill, we had to get out and push! Snow or anything on the line would stop it. The road in

The steam tram coming into Stony Stratford from Wolverton, *c.* 1914.

those days was twisty and turning. Where it turns to Old Wolverton, there was a sharp hill. If the tram hadn't got enough steam, he'd go bop, bop, bop and run back. We'd have to get out, push it over the top, get back in and away we'd go again. If it was wet, the driver would run it back nearly to Mill Drive, get up steam then go again, hoping he'd get over. Sometimes it would come off the rails and they'd back it on till it dropped on the metals and away it goes again.

Cecil Palmer

Lamplighter

The lamplighter came round at dusk, lighting the gas lamps with a long pole. My grandparents lived in Wolverton Road, Stony Stratford, and we'd sit in the window upstairs to see the people go by. Often we saw cattle being driven down the road to Canvin's the butchers to be slaughtered. A number of neighbours were regulars at the Jug and Bottle opposite – we could tell to the minute when each would emerge from their houses with their jugs to fetch beer for the evening. First Mrs Giles, then Mrs Jackson.

Audrey Lambert

Pumping water

At Wolverton, they kept all the horses at the fire station. If they got a fire alarm, they'd take the horses out, hook them onto the engine and they were away. They had a hand-pump with twelve men at each side pumping. They got water from the canal or wherever they could stop – ponds, canals or rivers.

Cecil Palmer

Quite alarming

We had our own fire brigade in Stony Stratford, in Silver Street. It was always fun to hear the whistle going, and the bell. We'd run to see how quick they'd turn out. There might have been a dozen volunteers for it. Mr Holland, the greengrocer, he'd down tools and off he'd go. Mr Yates, the captain, was always working round the back – he'd drop everything and run. Mr Braggins out of Wickens', he'd be there. The bell was on a pole by the fire station. They used to park lorries in the Square in the war, when it was open space. One night, at about one o'clock, my neighbour got his window open shouting, 'Fire! Fire! Fire!' A lorry was on fire just in front of us on the Square. He was stood there shaking. I tumbled downstairs, ran up Silver Street, broke the glass and fetched the fire engine. It was quite alarming really. I think it was only the cab got burnt. I lost a shoe running up Silver Street.

Arthur Cowley

Killed by design

When I came here from Pakistan in 1948, Wolverton was a throbbing, lovely working-class town with a high standard of education, high standard of further education. It had every religious denomination you could want. People came from all over just to come to Wolverton. It had a wonderful musical background. Down every street you had music teachers. Nearly every house had a piano. We had a brass band, flower shows, art shows and a wonderful cricket club which played in the Northants League and won many cups. Bowling clubs, tennis courts, we also had a lovely football club. And Milton Keynes came to kill it. They wanted all the grandness to go up there. Therefore they are killing us. The main artery, right in the middle of the main street, joined the bottom to the top, and they put the Agora in the middle there to stop the development of Wolverton. They wanted to

Market Square, Stony Stratford, in the 1940s.

kill Wolverton and they did it by design not by accident. They shut down the railway works by design and destroyed a wonderful building.

Clarence Vincent Gill

Brick wall

Wolverton was hemmed in by the brick wall at Wolverton Works and the streets. The mentality of Wolverton in all its aspects, in Church and everything else, was that of a brick wall.

Ron Staniford

Impoverished

Bletchley was a series of tin huts under the railway bridge and there was a cattle market where Sainsbury's is now. I liked the sheep. The Queen visited in 1966, so the High Street was renamed Queensway. Most of the shops were Victorian or Edwardian, with only the lower halves modernized. In the 1950s, they were traditional shops – the door in the centre, a counter each side, two display windows. I always felt Bletchley was an ugly place. The Brunel Centre was the first positive thing to happen, but it seems neglected. People were apathetic, there was an impoverished atmosphere. It never really had an identity. People were quite fearful when Milton Keynes was announced – a similar feeling when the Greater London Council started up the Lakes estate. I dislike the loss of the countryside, the loss of walks. Facilities are better now that Milton Keynes is here – the shops, the hospital. Walks are now better charted and more used. But I'm a Bletchley person, not MK.

Rosemary Evans

Bad egg publicity

The Lakes estate was a bit of a mix-up, frankly. The GLC [Greater London Council] planned it and grant-aided it but Bletchley Council was responsible for it. We carried the can for the Lakes estate. It got labelled because some people the GLC sent down were rogues they were glad to get rid of, members of a gang. Unfortunately, they got housed near each other. People who criticized the Lakes didn't realize there were 7,000 people there but it was the bad eggs that got all the publicity.

Ron Staniford

Tremendous community

I feel very defensive when the Lakes estate gets a negative press, because there is a tremendous community there – proved in 1990 when, it was very sad, a young girl of three was killed by a lorry going up the Stoke Road. Everyone was up in arms about it on the Lakes because they'd been on about the need for traffic calming. For a good six to eight weeks, every single day, hundreds of people turned up on that stretch of road at about five o'clock and blocked the road off. It was done in an organized way, with the co-operation of the police. They got the helicopter going to see these crowds of people. Within six months, the County Council found the money to put the traffic calming in.

Ken Beeley

Killed by expansion

Bletchley has gone down since MK, definitely in shopping. There used to be a Co-op wet-fish shop, a greengrocer's and butcher's but that has all gone now. Pedestrianization is not such a good thing for Bletchley. If there is no parking, people won't go. I think it will be like Fenny Stratford, killed by the expansion of Bletchley, and go the same way because of MK.

Brenda Monaghan

Stratford Road, Wolverton, 1935. The Old Bath House, now the headquarters of the Living Archive, is on the right by the bus stop.

Campaigning for the Fenny Stratford bypass, 1988.

Penned up

Fenny was bigger than Bletchley in the 1920s. The market was in Aylesbury Street. Cattle were penned up in the street. That's why the old pub there is called the Bull and Butcher. Bletchley had been so successful because of the nearby railway. It seems amazing today. Every Thursday, cattle market day, they'd drive the cattle up to the cattle dock onto trains for Birmingham or Islington. Chaps came from all around to buy cattle for slaughter.

Dicky Arnold

Good engines at Bletchley

I didn't know much about Bletchley – I fancied Peterborough and applied for a job there, but an old driver I knew told me how wonderful Bletchley was, because he liked his drink – he liked the Halfway House pub. He convinced me. There were some good engines at Bletchley, good tenders and tankers, and the *Royal Scot* went by. I ended up at Bletchley in March 1941.

Arthur Grigg

Open house

I was billeted during the war with my husband and small baby with Mrs MacBurnie in The Orchard in Far Bletchley, up the Buckingham road. She was aged ninety-two, a small white-haired lady wearing a long black skirt and long-sleeved white blouse. Round her neck was a small piece of velvet decorated by a brooch at the front. She had been a Court Dressmaker for Edward VII. Her orchard had plums, gages, blackcurrants, gooseberries, apples, vegetables. She kept open house for BP [Bletchley Park] workers who had been working all night and had missed breakfast.

Marjorie Chapman

Funny street

When I worked at Bletchley Park during the war, I was billeted in New Bradwell. it was one of those funny streets. I remember going in the wrong house when I first went there, they all looked the same.

Pamela O'Donahue

Special street

What's so special about Spencer Street, New Bradwell? Well, I've lived here twenty-two years. I'd grown up in a very tight-knit community where we didn't lock our doors and could knock on someone's door and say, 'Can I borrow some milk?' To me, that's what community is, and it isn't just in this street. You take it out of this street, you talk to your neighbours, you shop locally, you get to know people and build up trust with them. A few of us worked really hard at acknowledging local people and chatting to them. It helped having children going to school so you could talk to the mums.

Tina Strutton

Good neighbours

Next-door neighbours – we had some good laughs. Good neighbours. If you were skint, you could always go and borrow something, or they'd come and borrow off you. There was a lot of borrowing going on. Drop of milk, bit of sugar, bit of tea until tomorrow. That's how we used to live. Never looked back, never looked back since I came down to Bletchley, neither of us. We done well.

Ronald Flinn

Nice people

My married daughter lives in Milton Keynes and has four children. My wife kept coming to look after the grandchildren, spending a quarter of her time here, so we took this decision to move here. I was a bit worried but now we are pleased. The neighbours are nice people.

Donato Distazio

Wonderful neighbours

We've been very happy here [Bletchley]. We're just cemented here, you know. We've got some wonderful neighbours. The only time I think I might move is if I came into some money – I'd like to get a smallholding somewhere, but not far away, Stewkley, some-where like that.

Frank Bodimead

Moved to city centre

I do not think families are close today as when I was young. You might find the odd couple, families that are still living closely but before, you could walk down my road, and every other house would be Italian. Now there are two or three families left. They moved out of the area into the city centre.

Guiseppe Ciliberti

Heart-warming welcome

In the first year that we arrived in Milton Keynes, we were invited by my neighbour to go to her New Year's Eve party, and although I did not much enjoy the party, the heart-warming welcome by the host was a very nice, fresh and unforgettable experience for me.

Mr Wong

In the same boat

People were friendlier then. We helped each other. We'd go to jumble sales. We used to laugh about it – to see all this jumble stuff hanging on the line, but everybody was the same. We all made a joke of it but everybody was in the same boat.

Pat Flinn

No time to chat

In 1988, I moved to Milton Keynes from Liverpool, where the people were more approachable and friendly when compared with Milton Keynes. I wondered why my neighbours in Milton Keynes were so cool that we seldom met with each other. At last, I found that most of my neighbours used to work in London every day, so they spent lots of time travelling. They were so busy they had no time to chat.

Samuel Wong

Feelings were hurt

I discovered that local people are extreme – the nice one is a real gentleman, but the worst one is two-faced, underhand. I cut down two trees in front of my house because they were decayed by pests. When we passed by, we could not stand the pests falling down on us. Moreover, the trees were too tall and blocked the street lamp. My front door became a dark corner in the evening. So I sent a letter stating the reasons for cutting the trees to Milton Keynes Council. I never dreamed that a neighbour would accuse me of cutting the trees without asking his permission. Luckily I was approved, but I was never to speak to him any more. Before this argument, we were quite close – I not only used to go to the pub with him during the weekend, but also invited him and his girlfriend to come to my home for supper. My feelings were hurt. After that, I would never socialize with other people.

Tim Wong

A damned slacker!

'A damned slacker!' The repeated use of this term to Mr Percy Sykes, shopkeeper of Stantonbury, by the Reverend Guest, Vicar of Stantonbury, formed the principal bill of fare before the Newport Pagnell Bench on Wednesday 8 March . The reverend gentleman was summoned for applying this epithet as likely to lead to a breach of the peace under Byelaw 12, Buckinghamshire County Council. It appears there was bad blood between the two, which both denied, and that Mr Sykes had called the Vicar 'a cur' and 'a traitor to his Church'. The Bench decided the defendant must pay a £1 fine. The whole proceedings appeared rather farcical to your correspondent, except that behind it all there appeared a very unpleasant state of affairs in Church matters at Stantonbury.

The *Bucks Advertiser and Aylesbury News*, 11 March 1916

Working for the church

The Milton Keynes Chinese Christian Church was set up in 1990. Around thirty people, including the children, went to worship. Now the regular attendance at Sunday Worship is around 130 people. Because the majority of Christians in the church speak Cantonese, our Sunday Worship is in Cantonese as well. Our life is simple. I spend most of my free time working for the church at the children's Sunday school.

Samuel Wong

The lunch club

Social workers asked us to look for the elderly in the community. So my friend and myself went house-to-house, calling on people and asking if they had elderly parents or in-laws, what illness they suffer from, are they mobile or not. We started up a lunch club – the Dosti Lunch Club. We are in the seventh year now.

Pushpa Pandit

Many projects

There was a policy that Milton Keynes Development Corporation would fund a project for three years on a sliding scale, so you could establish yourself. That didn't mean you were left floundering at the end – there were many eggs in the basket and many grants. Inter Action were only one of many, many projects instigated. I think the Corporation did a damn good job and they supported us as much as they possibly could.

Tracy Walters

Working really hard

We have the Great Linford Festival and people are working really hard for that. We're going to celebrate Great Linford 2001 because this is the real millennium. That has brought a lot of people together. We had an Indian meal in the memorial hall two weeks ago and it was a wonderful occasion. A lot of money will go to 'Phoenix XXXXX', the new hospice for young people. They're having a competition to design a bit of the green. You can pay some money towards it or work on it.

Kathy Baker

Lifelong friendships

The Queen's Jubilee was something special in Milton Keynes. Lifelong friendships came out

Children enjoying games at the Coffee Hall Community Workshop in 1984.

The residents of Oxford Street, Wolverton, celebrate winning a cake for being the best-dressed street for the Coronation in 1953.

of that weekend. We laid tables out for the children, there was some music, and the adults had a party in the evening. But it was such a bonding for people to meet one another. Roads were inviting other roads along. I'm not a Royalist – we had quite a few radical views – but when it came to this particular day, it broke the barriers down. The only other time I've seen a neighbourhood come together again was when the Princess died. We have to have an excuse like that in England to let out our emotions. It either has to be a good party or a good funeral.

Tina Strutton

Getting involved

My son was taken ill – he had a hernia and you suddenly realize that there wasn't a hospital in Milton Keynes. The slogan that went on at the time was 'Everybody's dying for a hospital' and I joined the Hospital Action Group and got involved with that.

Ken Beeley

The best place

Milton Keynes is the best place for disabled and elderly people. It is the best place. Everywhere there is access to disabled. And the GPs and consultants are very concerned about my life. I was very young to be landed into bed and be disabled and they gave me the best treatment. I always want to work for other people, be a volunteer of some sort, so I joined a club called Dial for disabled people.

Pushpa Pandit

Treated as an equal

On the first day at work [at Milton Keynes Development Corporation], I arrived in this great open-plan office and they said, 'This is your boss, Barry Clayton'. My first thought was, 'I can't possibly call him Barry'. Because the way we were brought up – I was nineteen then – you called nobody by their Christian name unless they were contemporaries. Adult friends of Mum and Dad were called Auntie or Uncle. Everybody else was called Mr, Mrs or Miss. That was a real life change for me. All these people treated me as an equal – I'd just come out of college and was just plunged into this. And it was lovely.

Sue Malleson

Crazy move

My friends in London thought I was crazy, moving to Milton Keynes. They couldn't understand why I'd decided to do it. I felt like a rat leaving the sinking ship because I'd been very vocal in opposing the closure of the school I was in. It was a lovely place, a really happy school, so I felt like I was deserting.

Debbie Greaves

Quieter living

I'd lived in Luton for eighteen and a half years and it was getting a bit scrappy with violence. I hoped for a quieter living and a better schooling for the children in Milton Keynes. I must confess I did like it. My favourite place

Trustees of the Margaret Powell Foundation formally opening the theatre concourse in 2000. It was named after a wealthy Milton Keynes landowner, in recognition of the Foundation's support for the disabled and the elderly.

is home – I make it comfortable for myself and do my garden because when I'm down here I speak to the flowers and I think best. I speak to the trees. They don't answer back.

Neville Rose

Such good friends

If two Chinese families had not helped us on our first arrival, we wouldn't have been living in Milton Keynes for ten years. I can hardly imagine living here without their help. Although my wife is Christian, I am not. I wonder how everything seems to be arranged. Is it God? I am so lucky to have such good friends that I really want to say thank you to them from the bottom of my heart. They are our main supporters. I will never forget them in all my life.

Chun Yau Leung

A caring place

I have met some super people, people with qualities I admire and try to emulate. It's been a caring place to live, and I know that more than most. I've felt it lots of times in my life. I've just been enfolded in a nice cosy blanket and I think that's how I would sum up Milton Keynes. As a nice place to live.

Norma Jamieson

Wolverton Sponsored Walk, 1982.

nine
Unforgettable Moments, Memorable People

Garden Court in Central Milton Keynes, 1979, later renamed Queen's Court after HRH Queen Elizabeth II's visit to the city later that year.

Bare-breasted girls

New Bradwell's rather a small place – there's one row of shops. This man came along and dared to open a shop for gentlemen with bare-breasted girls as hairdressers. Oh I mean! I thought it was entirely the wrong place for it. But we laughed like mad. One morning, they had the girl who was the hairdresser on television and she was saying she couldn't understand people being funny about it. They asked viewers what they thought of it. I rang up and funny enough I got through. I said I didn't really object to the shop as such but that New Bradwell wasn't the place. I said, 'We could have a tit for tat!' Of course, I went along to the shop and said, 'If there's a top-less shop for men, would you be prepared to have a bottomless shop for the ladies?' He lasted three months.

June Shrewsbury

Tissues and orange peel

When we were acquiring land [for MKDC], I drove in my little Mini car up the old lane from the Woolstones. It went down to a track, but I had to get to this site which was farmland. It was a lovely hot summer's day. I got to the top and suddenly, out of the corner of my eye, I saw this Range Rover and two naked people picnicking. I kept my eyes resolutely looking forward and drove past them to the site that I was going to inspect. It's been a constant regret ever since that I never looked properly. I left it a reasonable amount of time, turned round and came back, by which time, of course, they'd gone and all that was left was tissues and orange peel.

Bob Hill

Tea bags and matches

[At Inter Action], we used to do things with Stantonbury [Campus] when they had their 'Day Ten'. We'd give students a tea bag, a tin can and a box of matches. They'd have to cross the Grand Union Canal on their own steam – work out how to do it, use teamwork, get to the other side, find some water, make a cup of tea and then get back again. Well, you wouldn't dare do that sort of project any more.

Sue Burrows

War games

I was a police cadet in the police station in Simpson Road, Bletchley, in 1957. One day, we went up to Brickhill Woods to do a war games exercise. We were the quarry, and that was really frightening. You'd leg it into the woods and hide and when they found you they were quite naughty. I mean, they took it too far. You were only seventeen-, eighteen-year-old kids – you were meat and drink to them. I'd still got the 'mod' mentality, still bombing around on my Lambretta scooter, still associating with the kids I'd always been with. And someone in CID would come up to me and say, 'You know so-and-so, don't you?' I'd say, 'Yeah, play football with him.' 'Well, watch him – you're not supposed to be hanging around with him.'

Stephen Flinn

Still drinking

You can imagine, being Italian, how big a football supporter I am. I played at quite a high level in Italy as a semi-professional. I played football until I was thirty-five in this country, with North Bucks and MK League – for Woburn, Bletchley and various towns. One day, we went to play football in Olney. When we finished, we stopped for a drink, only one drink because our wives were wait-ing at home. Instead it came to four o'clock and we were still drinking. The wives got a

The Wolverton-Stony Stratford steam tram getting stuck in floods in the 1920s.

bit agitated and contacted the police to see if we'd had an accident on the road. On the way back, we had to stop to go to the toilet. We jumped over the hedge, got back in and drove off. When we got back to the village, we were all told off by our wives for being late. But one of the players was missing – we'd left him there, drunk behind the hedge, and this poor girl, his wife, was going raving mad because her husband had not come back!

Donato Piselli

Whooooomft!

We were digging this manhole shaft down at the Barge in Simpson, about six metres in diameter, going down twenty-five or thirty foot. We spent three days putting a ladder bay in it when we hit rock – you've got to blast it. Well, I'm no explosives expert, but I was in the TA. We started drilling this rock and putting explosives in. When I looked down, I thought, 'He's putting a bloody lot of explosives in there!' So I jumped in the car and backed it down the field. The next minute – whooooomft! There were bits of ladder, everything came flying out of this shaft and everyone was running like mad. The shaft started filling up with water, right up to the top. I got the pump and put it into a little pond – right opposite the Barge. Two o'clock Saturday morning, there's a knock at the door. It's the police. First thing, you think is somebody's been killed or hurt – it frightened the life out of me. They said, 'Are you the engineer in charge of the shaft down at Simpson?' I said, 'Yes'. They said, 'Well, can you come and turn the bloody pump off because all the beer's floating around in the cellar of the Barge!'

Brian O'Sullivan

Just stick with it

I remember standing by the side of the road watching those huge road-building machines,

A train crash at Bletchley on Friday 13 October 1939.

huge land-movers – with two young lads in a buggy absolutely going ga-ga over this wonderful machinery. I'm standing there cold and wet and miserable and muddy thinking, 'They're loving this. Just stick with it a bit longer.'

Annie Bradstock

Up to the neck in mud

When we first came up here in 1972, the only work was building work. That was good because you got priority housing. We got this house, went round and looked at it and said, 'Wow, nail the front door up – we're in. You're not getting us out!' We couldn't believe it. It was a brand new house, just cleaned up from the builders. The garden was stuck up to the neck in mud. The fence was just one piece of wire slung on three posts, one against the house, one half-way down the garden and one at the bottom. There was an orchard behind us full of rats. It was a wrench moving away, but, oh God,

it was exciting! It was a total start. We were moving into a field. There was just two blocks of houses around us, in the middle of fields. We stood there and said, 'What have we done?'

David Webb

Driving with one leg

Moving day was traumatic because I broke my leg playing football in London. It delayed our departure – I was in plaster from ankle to thigh. But we'd given notice on the flat we was in so we had to move. I actually drove the removal van. Borrowed one from a friend of mine and drove it from London to Milton Keynes myself. It was quite dramatic trying to drive with one leg in plaster.

John Staniland

Mattresses on the floor

It was awful on moving day. We couldn't afford proper removals so Ken hired a small van and we did it in stages. The house was full of plastic bags. There was no carpets. Three-storey house, nothing in it. Then I got a phone call to say they'd broken down in Toddington service station. So myself and two daughters did the first night on mattresses on the floor and I remember crying and thinking, 'Oh God, what have I done?'

June Shrewsbury

Out on a limb

I had all my three children at the Whalley Drive Maternity Unit. The first two were fine. The third one was slightly worrying because my waters had broken and they said, 'Right – we're going to give you this injection and get this baby on the way because, if not, we're going to stick you in an ambulance to Aylesbury. The thought of travelling to Aylesbury while in labour was not much fun – you did feel a bit out on a limb. To have the hospital now within ten minutes is pure bliss.

Sue Malleson

We thought it was cool

I was one of the children in the [MKDC] red balloon advert when I was about nine years old. The whole school was involved. We went to the Bowl – I remember a teacher explaining about the Bowl. All the schools were there. We thought it was cool! We had a couple of practice runs, letting go of the balloons at the right time and then they filmed it. I made sure I was at the front so I could see myself on telly – I wore bright pink! It lasted all day.

Samantha Bassnett

I was absolutely terrified

Anglia Television decided to do a documentary about Milton Keynes, called *The Making of a*

Young labourers at Great Linford, 1978.

City and asked me, my husband and two children to make the film with them. It went out live at Stantonbury Theatre and there was a big debate afterwards with the Development Corporation. They filmed us in our accommodation in London and said, 'This is a typical London family that are taking the plunge and moving to Milton Keynes'. They filmed us after we moved into Tinkers Bridge, and at the Leisure Centre at Bletchley, swimming. They filmed us on Dial-a-Bus – a sort of public transport. I was absolutely terrified, but really it was a wonderful experience.

Kathy Sellick

I will never forget it in all my life

I worked in a factory. Most of the labourers were local people. Some were black, and I was the only Chinese. At first I felt strange and lonely because the local people here talk always in slang – it was totally different from formal English. I didn't know what they were talking about and they were difficult to approach as well. However, the black people were very nice and friendly. They always cared for me. After I had settled down, I was getting on better with the local people. Some of them spoke slower in order to let me know what they were talking about. At last I discovered that all of them were very nice, very straight and childlike. They liked playing and joking. After I had resigned and said farewell to them, I hardly imagined they would all line up and give me a present, which was a ball pen. I was amazed. That emotional moment was one of my unforgettable experiences. I will never forget it in my life.

Peggy Yee

Old boys

Scotsmen, Irishmen, Welshmen, Englishmen – people from all over England came to Milton Keynes to work. They were all smashing people. There was a local bloke called Harry from Woburn Sands, a carpenter. I worked with him on Tinkers Bridge and used to sit with him in the canteen. He had a funny North Bucks accent which was quite unique. One day, we were sitting in the canteen talking and he said, 'I had a lot of trouble last night, these old boys on motorbikes riding up and down.' I had a picture in my mind of all these old-age pensioners on motorbikes. I said, 'Was it a motorcycle club or something?' He said, 'No, the old boys who live locally'. I said, 'What – on motorbikes? What age are they?' He said, 'Oooh, seventeen or eighteen'. I said, 'They're young boys!' He said, 'No, we call them old boys!'

Brian O'Sullivan

A mass of men

I remember when I first started work as a junior reporter on the *Wolverton Express*, the lunchtime signal would go and a mass of men would be walking up the streets with their bags for lunch. And it would go again and they'd go back in. Deserted – some of the shops used to shut. Absolutely amazing.

Sue Burrows

The old days

I was twelve at the time the Deanshanger Iron Works was burnt in 1912. I went over with two of my brothers. We saw the fire engine come through Wolverton, it was horse-drawn. Then Stony Stratford fire station got there first. My brothers and I went tearing across the fields and were there to see the roof fall in. I was a special policeman from 1926 to 1948. Sergeant Rollings, my boss, was a huge man – twenty-two stone, about six foot three. He was a lovely sergeant. We had points to go to, either a telephone kiosk at the top of the town or up at the garage in London Road or Calverton Road or Old Stratford river bridge. You'd got to be there at a certain time and somebody would meet you and say, 'Everything OK?' And you'd go your separate ways to the next point.

Cecil Palmer

Unforgettable school days

18 September 1913: An aeroplane passed over the school about 2.15 p.m. I let all the children, in charge of their teachers, watch its flight from the playground.

23 September 1913: An army airship passed over the school this morning. The children had a good view of it from the playground. Seventy-five absent in the afternoon. Nearly all had been taken by their parents to Stony Stratford to see the soldiers.

20 September 1914: Was sorry to hear that Hilda Callow, a little girl in the Third Class, met with a fatal accident when going home from school yesterday afternoon. She fell in the road and was crushed by the wheels of a

Wolverton Works employees, photographed by Bob Jardine on 18 May 1984 as part of 'Day in the Life', Living Archive's exhibition of photography and reminiscence.

heavy wagon. I am constantly warning the children of the danger of playing in the road.

Elizabeth Ainge, in charge of the Infants' Department, New Wolverton British School

When the siren went

The first time a siren went, we were delivering bread in the High Street. What did we do? We came home with the horse and put it right in the stable. After a while, we didn't take any notice of it.

Arthur Cowley

The farmers

Ted Norman used to take me shooting. I weren't very old. I think I was five. We went up one field and he shot a rabbit and its head were dragging on the ground. He kept saying, 'Pick it up, my man, pick it up'. When I got home, he gave me the rabbit. The only time he frightened me was when I'd been out with

him shooting and his gun kept pointing at me. I was glad when we got back. He was a bit drunk. Mr Lucket was a bit strict. He said anybody fall out with him, he'd be like a steamroller and knock them down. A big bloke he were. He wasn't very popular.

Joseph Willis

The vicar

The vicar was noted for giving generously, usually food, to tramps. They had their own sign language, which they chalked on the wall outside to tell their friends it was a good house to call at.

Audrey Lambert

The undertaker

Gurney was the undertaker in New Bradwell. You could always tell when someone had died because Gurney would put on his black hat. There was a legend that when a black crow

The opening of Milton Keynes central railway station by HRH Prince Charles on 14 May 1982.

landed on Gurney's roof, he would know that someone had died and he would put on his hat and go up and down the little alleyways at the back of the houses until someone came out and said, 'Mr Gurney, we need your services'.

Tina Strutton

All drawed up

I was born on 30 March 1917 in No. 3 Brookfield Cottages, Old Bradwell. My mum came from Earls Barton, near Wellingborough. She died Christmas Eve when I was thirteen. Her hands were all drawed up. They said it was rheumatism. She was only about forty-six.

Joseph Willis

Always drawn down

My father never did any more work [as a wheelwright at the Wolverton Works] from 1918 till he died in 1939. He had an operation

in London. They had to take a length of his gut out and he was always drawn down. He couldn't lift a bucket of water or anything.

Cecil Palmer

Be a family still

I remember, when I was twelve years old, my mum actually asking me how I felt about my parents divorcing and I remember crying and saying, 'Please don't divorce – I want us to be a family still!' And three years later, they did separate and I was very glad. My dad was an incredibly traditionally-minded Indian man – with the Zoroastrian culture, whereby the woman should stay at home and look after the kids, not go to work, not really have a voice on important issues. But mum was always the one to go out to work – being the strong character that she is, she has broken many taboos. In Kenya, she had been a secretary with major companies.

Soraya Billimoria

A children's party at Wolverton Infants' School (now Wyvern School), *c.* 1935.

Bitter experience

I was seriously homesick in the first year after we moved to Milton Keynes. Maybe I am an emotional and sentimental person because I hid and cried my eyes out and I didn't let my daughter know. Two years ago, I was told that my grandmother in her nineties had passed away. She was so dear to me because she had brought me up in my early age when my mum went to work. We were very close and I loved her so deeply that I grieved for her death. This was my bitter experience.

Connie Yuen

My grandmother was a terror

My grandmother was a terror. Everybody said she was a terror. When she was looking after the shop and a stranger came in that wasn't a regular customer and asked for a bag of flour, which they didn't sell a lot of, she'd say to them, 'You go and buy your flour where you buy your bread!' She was very rude and abrupt. She was a real Pomeranian. Mind you, she had eleven children.

Arthur Cowley

My grandad was wonderful

I was really close to my grandad but he had a stroke and he could not speak. He could just about say my name. He was a very independent man. He would never catch the bus but walk everywhere, even to the city. Mum would be at work, as was my dad, and we were at school. By the time we all got home, he would have ironed the clothes and cleaned the house. It was really good having him come to live with us. He was wonderful. I think I reminded him of his daughter who died when she was four, so he'd really make a fuss of me.

Anon

An amazing man

Jock Campbell [Lord Campbell of Eskan, MKDC Chairman, 1967-1983] was an amazing man. He was charm itself. He was an old Etonian, a socialist peer, a trustee of Chequers, so he knew Mrs Thatcher well. And yet, because of his experience working for the family firm, Booker McConnell – he'd been sent to the West Indies as a young man and had seen the kind of conditions the workers on the estates had been living in – he had a very passionate view on the importance of social housing. So he brought all that, plus his love of the arts, plus his kind of humanity. He was a wily old bird too.

Roger Kitchen

He wasn't having it

Jock Campbell's whole attitude was that it was going to be a City of Trees and he wasn't having any of this business of solid slabs of concrete here and there.

Henry Dewick

A tremendous humanitarian

Fred Lloyd Roche [MKDC General Manager, 1971-1980] made the city happen. He was a tremendous humanitarian. He believed in design for people and for quality of life, not in design for the architectural professional's self-admiration. He had a terrific understanding of the value of landscape but he also had a real sense of humanity. He was a really good spotter of talent and he found a way of enabling that talent.

Neil Higson

In and out in a minute

Fred Lloyd Roche came to a meeting, very early on, in Wolverton. We were very concerned about four-inch kerbs on the cycleways, which were terrible. Every time you came to a junction on the bicycle, you had to get off. We were very upset about this. Fred came and said, 'I've read your reports and I agree and will instruct my officers to drop all the kerbs'. He was in and out in a minute. We were astonished we'd got what we wanted.

Philip Ashbourn

The Emperor

Lloyd Roche was a brilliant bloke. There ought to be a memorial to him. If he hadn't been in charge, the new city wouldn't have been built so well or so quickly. The farmers called him the Emperor because he had the 'power of life or death'. I got to know him really well. I'd go and see him if I had a problem and he would always listen. I also had a lot to do with Alan Ashton, the Development Corporation Estates Officer, regarding the acquisition of land and planning of the new city – he had a really good team. He died in 1976, before he finished his job.

Dicky Arnold

I felt as if I had been hit

When I was at school, corporal punishment was still around. The teacher used to smack you around the head if you were out of order. Your ears would ring and your head would spin. I remember walking up the hill towards Wolverton – there was no city centre or hospital then – and I was shopping, Saturday morning shop, and it hit me like that, 'I am going to put roots down in this place called Milton Keynes'. I felt as if I had been hit. It didn't hurt. It was just my head spinning. It was a realization of self-belief and self-confidence, which I hadn't felt in years. Somehow this was the place where I could turn myself around. It was up to me. I could either blow it or turn it into something that was a way of life.

Tracy Walters

ten
Changing
Worlds

Polling Day, May 1891. Campaigning for the Liberal
candidate for Bletchley Park, Herbert Leon.

It's hard to change

It's hard to change but, when you're faced with it, you accept and adapt. It's not good being a farmer in the middle of a city. It's different but we manage. There's a lot of public wandering about. There's a horse track through it – you get people riding horses, people picnicking and a bit of dog trouble with the sheep as well. Twenty-five years on, I suppose Milton Keynes is good for a lot of people but not for anyone interested in farming. In some ways, the land-scaping and parks have been managed well but the park as it is now – they won't allow me to spray it and it's a mass of thistles. They say it might kill some other plants and wild flowers. They don't really want me to put fertilizer on it either. They are not interested in farming and just want people like me to graze it so they don't have to keep mowing it.

Tony King

Big and tall now

I'm gobsmacked when I look round at the landscaping now, especially the trees at Kiln Farm, which were like twigs when I put them in. They are so big and tall now. I feel proud to have been part of it. Milton Keynes is beautiful. The best part is in spring when all the bulbs come up. The idea was to drive through Milton Keynes and not realize you'd been through a city. That's certainly succeeded. Coming to Milton Keynes was the best thing that could have happened to me.

Mick Kelly

Live and let live

When we heard this place was going to be developed, well, it was terrible. But we couldn't have got into farming if the city hadn't have come. It's enabled us to rent land

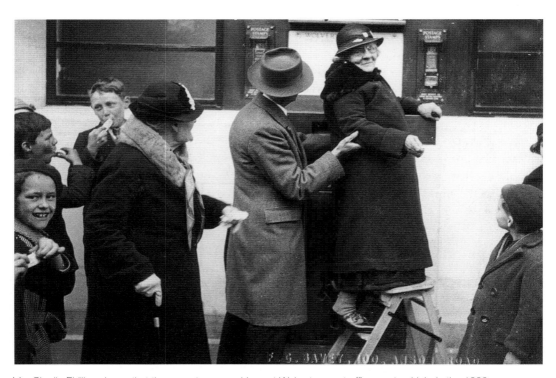

Mrs Charlie Phillips shows that the new stamp machines at Wolverton post office are too high, in the 1930s.

at a reasonable rate. We've been treated very well by the Development Corporation – after the beginning, when they were going round drilling holes everywhere to see the soil. We bloomin' well had lambs drown in them boreholes, cattle with broken legs. Well, after the initial upset, it's not as bad as we thought it would be. You've got to live and let live. At one time, if people were on your land, you went with a shotgun and told them to clear off. You don't nowadays. If people are blackberrying along the hedge, well, why not. Wandering around the fields to pick fresh mushrooms – it's lovely, nice. Never mind seeing folk around as long as they respect what you've got. The general public and the farming community can live very well side by side. Farmers love to talk to them about this, that and the other 'cos it's a lonely life, farming.

Sam and Pam Sinfield

The first passenger coach

My father learnt his trade at Judge's wheelwrights. He'd build horse traps as well as bicycles, not motor cars, for there were none about. Then he was wheelwright in the Works and used to do all of the bodywork. He built the first horse-drawn passenger coach for the railway that went to and from Euston station. All the horse-drawn vehicles for the LNWR were built at Wolverton.

Cecil Palmer

One-person vehicles

The only time there's a traffic jam in Milton Keynes are the rush hours – 95 per cent of the vehicles have one person in them. That must be the challenge: what sort of incentives do you need for people to car-share?

Brian Salter

I'm not having this!

I'd take all the kids, when they got to my house, down to Simpson School. That was when the earthmovers were doing the balancing lakes. I got soaked, I got drenched. The lorries were going along the road, just splashing us. I said, 'I'm not having any of this!' I rang up MKDC. They wouldn't let the children walk any more, got transport to take them because they did see the danger.

Sandra Page

Live poultry

The railway carrier always delivered large items which had come by rail in a horse-drawn wagon. Also live chickens, ducklings, goslings – which my mother ordered from a firm in Norfolk – were labelled 'live poultry' and had to be delivered within twenty-four hours.

Audrey Lambert

The Nightrider

In the early years of the new city, you could buy a return ticket to London for 25p – the British Rail Nightrider – from about 4 p.m, last train back at 12.20 a.m. It was much used and indicated that extended families were still largely in London. You could get the train from Wolverton and Bletchley.

Norma Jamieson and Carole Loxton

Big old wagons

We had big old wagons – four-wheeled ones with wooden sides and reins up the front. And we bought some of the old railway drays and made them bigger and they done as wagons – solid, like. We had one from old Tilley's [Wolverton toy factory] that weighed a couple of ton without anything on it.

Joseph Willis

Dial-a-bus

MKDC introduced the Dial-a-bus system. Outside your houses were like lamp-posts with a phone on it. You'd press a button and say, 'Right, can I have a bus to Bletchley, outside No. 21, one adult, two children. And they used to come right outside your house. It was magic. It worked really well, but it obviously wasn't profitable because it didn't last long.

Kathy Sellick

Never rode, they walked

People used to live and work and walk in the area they lived in. They never rode, they walked, and that's what made them more noticeable to the things around them. You get in your car and drive off to the city centre but you never see nothing. But if you walked, you'd see a lot more, wouldn't you? You would.

Bernard Groom

Iron wheels

We had one of the very first tractors, a Fordson with no mudguards. It was very dangerous because, if you left the plough in the ground, if you weren't careful, it would bring the front of the tractor up. They reckon there was a lot of blokes been killed like that. It used to have iron wheels and clank going up them cobbles with the old mower. Then the big end went.

Joseph Willis

Taxis are a way of life

Transport is a very difficult thing in the city, for young people in particular. Public transport has been expensive for going anywhere at night-time. Taxis are a way of life for people in Milton Keynes.

Sue Burrows

The wheel shop at Wolverton Works, 1984.

High Street, Stony Stratford, *c*. 1900.

Norman the Butcher in Wolverton, *c*. 1910.

Convenient for driving

I was bewildered by the roundabouts. They made me lose my way. Then I discovered that the grid design, special in Milton Keynes, was how to find things. Because there were only a few traffic lights in the centre, it was very convenient for driving.

Samuel Wong

A dreadful road

There are 200 miles of roads in Milton Keynes. The road between Milton Keynes and Aylesbury is a dreadful road. That is not an accident. That is a political reality because Aylesbury was terrified, with some justification, that a huge new city centre in Milton

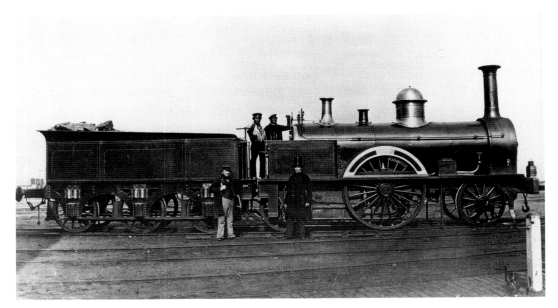

The *Osprey*, a Wolverton Bloomer-class engine, 1880s. The man in the top hat is Mr Widdowson, the LNWR Paymaster. A replica of the *Osprey* stands in Station Square outside Milton Keynes central railway station.

Sir Peter Parker, British Rail chairman (right) with HRH Prince Charles (back view) at the naming of the *City of Milton Keynes* engine on 14 May 1982.

Keynes would vacuum all the money out of South Bucks. North Bucks was a kind of rural, flat, fog-ridden backwater. They weren't interested in North Bucks. Then, all of a sudden, they had this huge project that they had to fund in many respects – schools, libraries – so they were very stiff about it.

John Napleton

The frozen north

When I first came here, they said to me, 'Oh, you're going to the frozen north?' I said, 'What do you mean?' And they said, 'Well, you'll find out when you get there'. And when I came here, I found that the county ended at Aylesbury, in effect. South Bucks and Aylesbury was the county. North of that was frozen – nothing went on hardly.

Ernest Pye

Fighting in the streets

Stony has always been a Conservative stronghold and even the working man votes Conservative. Wolverton is different. It's a railway town, but Stony was here before the railway. In 1908, the election was fought between Freemantle, Conservative and Verney, Liberal. Freemantle got in and, when it was declared at night, there was fighting in the streets. As soon as the fighting started, the policeman came walking up. They scattered everywhere and that was the end of it.

Cecil Palmer

Old-style MP

In 1964, a Tory guy, Sir Frank Markham, was the 'sitting tenant' – the old style of MP. He wasn't seen and nothing was known about him. Then along comes Robert Maxwell.

Alan Marshall

Captain Bob

Captain Bob wore a British uniform and a medal he'd won in the war. He came across as genuine. He had trouble with the Wolverton Labour party – perhaps his wife had upset them. But I found them nice people. In 1968, I couldn't get a house and then went to see him, and within a fortnight I'd got a flat. I thought all the trouble was a smear campaign at first. I thought he did good in the area. He was MP, then Bill Benyon won the seat back.

Gordon Marshall

We had Maxwell rumbled

Of course, when Maxwell came, he completely destabilized the place. We had Maxwell rumbled early on. He promised to buy Pullman the printers in Bletchley and employ about 200 people but, after he was elected, no more was heard. He'd parade about in Bletchley. We weren't surprised when Pergamon Press went up the chute. He always referred to himself as 'the printing millionaire' but he wasn't.

Dicky Arnold

Paternalistic socialism

What attracted me to Milton Keynes was a very paternalistic socialism, because it helped people. I'd worked in London housing areas before I came and I was astonished at what poor conditions people had to live in. It was an eye-opener for me, and I'd travelled the world. I'd been to Calcutta but I still found it astonishing working in Battersea in the early seventies. So a lot of people came here. It was a very exciting time because they did get new opportunities. Younger people came up and they settled here and sent for their parents, their grandparents.

Philip Ashbourn

Shared aspirations

The Development Corporation, on the whole, was run by people who had shared aspirations, who wanted to see Milton Keynes as a success and its success is largely down to those people – who fought for the fact that you needed an open market in the city centre, that you needed community facilities in the local areas, that the Redways were driven by a desire to make a better place in which to live. Their loyalties and their drive were about Milton Keynes.

Debbie Greaves

Ideas of Utopia

All such people [early MKDC settlers] were here because they really cared. They had ideas of Utopia and really wanted it to happen. The good thing about moving in new was that so many people were brand new, nobody knew anything. You felt you had the right to get involved because there weren't 'old soldiers' doing it. It was easy to get involved if you wanted to. You developed new skills yourself.

Norma Jamieson

I miss that sort of thing

The population of Bradwell village was 391. Now it is approximately 3,000. People were really annoyed when property was beginning to be built. You'd know everyone in the village. You don't now and I miss that sort of thing, and the animals. In certain ways, I am very sorry that Milton Keynes has been built, but the city has certainly been well done.

Ron Perry

British decadence

We hear a good deal nowadays about British decadence and effeminacy. Showers of letters are rained on the press, deploring the weakness and faddishness of the rising male generation. They say England is going to the dogs. It is quite true that one can hardly walk for 100 yards in the town without meeting some pale, sickly, ill-formed specimen of manhood. But, in nine cases out of ten, his condition is the result of the conditions of life under which he has grown from boyhood. Nowadays, with laws of fresh air in the home, and medical inspection in schools, we are going a long way towards building a foundation of national life, where the weedy specimen will be the exception and not the rule.

Wolverton Express, 24 April 1914

Different type of people

I'm extremely proud of Milton Keynes now and what it's done. I think the people of Milton Keynes are a completely different type of people – even our third- and fourth-generation kids coming up now are different. They'll have a go at anything and everybody will try and do something different and help each other to try and make it succeed. This is what the buzz is within Milton Keynes itself, it really is. It was the greatest move I ever did, to come here. Milton Keynes is my adopted city and I'm more than proud and will tell anybody, anywhere that if they want a great life, if they're prepared to put anything into Milton Keynes, they'll get a great deal out of it. It's a fantastic place.

Ken Beeley

We are all foreigners in MK

Due to the sense of superiority of native-born people, racism is a common phenomenon in Britain. But I don't think it is as common here as in other cities because there were not many native-born people in Milton Keynes.

Most people seemed to be moving in from somewhere else. It can be said that we are all foreigners in Milton Keynes.

Samuel Wong

Everything we want

Milton Keynes is absolutely wonderful. We've got that theatre, we've got everything we want. We've got the shops – you don't have to go to London, you've got it on your doorstep. The planning of the greenery – it's beautiful. To see Milton Keynes as it is, I'm proud to be a part of it, especially when you see that beautiful cathedral.

Sandra Page

A fantastic place

Milton Keynes is a fantastic place. I owe Milton Keynes a lot. I've worked my life here and enjoyed it . There's some fantastic people. It's educated my three children. I've got one at university, which I don't think would have happened if I'd stayed where I was – not down in Richmond. I've got one who's doing quite well in the army, and my son's put back into Milton Keynes basically what we've taken. He's worked at the hospital since he left school, about ten years. Milton Keynes is a fantastic place. I would never decry it. The people who make jokes about it have never been here.

Brian O'Sullivan

A personal attachment

I've lived all over the country. I came to Milton Keynes in 1972 when I was twenty-five. I'd say that my own personal growth has been in parallel with the city – I somehow feel interlinked with it, affected by it, joined with it, and so I do have a very personal attachment to this place. It's a sense of home. It's more a home than any place I've ever lived.

Kathy Chapman

Not constrained by history

We have a great infrastructure. If you have lived in Milton Keynes for a while, the thing that really makes you appreciate it is going into another town. Everything is inconvenient there. You get stuck in traffic jams. You cannot park anywhere. You cannot find your way to places. Here it is so easy. We have so much green land as well. We love going to the parkland around the lake – everything is accessible. Within a month or two of living in Milton Keynes, we made more friends than in all the time we were in Houghton Regis. There are so many interesting people – it is a rich and interesting and forward-looking culture. Milton Keynes embraces a new and different way of living. When I look at the city centre, the developments there are all wonderful. They remind me of when we lived in Madras, which is vibrant, lots of interesting things to do. You have a feeling of life. You are not constrained by history stopping you doing things.

Ravi Fernandez

The place is teeming

We have more access to green and countryside now, because many of the places were private. Where the city centre was built was Bradwell Common, which was fiercely guarded by gamekeepers – access was not allowed. Shenley Wood was huge fields, now covered by trees. There's more wildlife here than when it was intensively farmed, certainly more birdlife, certainly more waterbirds – the place is teeming.

Tracy Walters

Cyclists in Milton Keynes' Linear Park, 2003. (courtesy of Milton Keynes Park Trust)

I get a buzz

I always get a buzz when I read or hear people defending Milton Keynes. I love to hear people speak well of it. I get a buzz now when I hear people in the theatre. What I get most joy out of is people thinking they made the right decision to come here.

Bob Hill

A pretty good job

I was one of Milton Keynes' biggest critics when they talked of it coming here but, when I look around, I think MKDC have done a pretty good job. I mean, I talk to lots of people that come to this area and they're absolutely amazed at what there is for people here.

David Bodley

What it needs now

Milton Keynes is bloody marvellous as it is but it's still growing and that original level of imagination and dynamism is what it needs

now. And it needs the enthusiasm and the preparedness to gamble and the commitment to people with slightly odd ideas. It's a great place.

Neil Higson

The sense of freedom

I like the Redways most of all: the sense of freedom, of being able to cycle around surrounded by landscape and see people at work, children at school, people in their homes. That sums up Milton Keynes for me. I'm very proud to be here. I'm a fierce defender of it and, if people make critical remarks about it, I'm afraid I've ignored them or I'm very abrupt with them.

William Slee

Funding nightmare

We may not have appreciated the Corporation and their largesse as much as we should have done. But we certainly miss it now. Having to find funding for arts projects is a nightmare. You're only secure for a year at a time and we're increasingly having to look outside local authorities and regional arts boards to keep going. It's sad because community arts organizations reach an awful lot of people who may be excluded from other avenues. And it's much, much more bureaucratic – health and safety is extremely good but it's also time-consuming and costly.

Sue Burrows

Only in Great Britain

It's always amazed me that only in Great Britain would you find media knocking an achievement like Milton Keynes. You go anywhere else in the world, they've heard of Milton Keynes. They love it! They're copying bits of it. It appears in Japanese kids' textbooks. We have nothing to be ashamed of.

John Napleton

A train hitting the buffers

Margaret Thatcher decreed that new town development corporations would be discontinued. Frank Henshaw [MKDC General Manager 1983-1992] said, 'Come 1992, we can liken the Development Corporation to an express train hitting the buffers at ninety miles an hour. The bits will be scattered all over the place. The line should continue for many more miles.' There was an awful lot more work to be done; it was sad that the principles that had been in operation for such a long time were not allowed to continue for longer.

Malcolm Anderson

The death throes

The end was coming up and I was quite cross about that because our work at MKDC was nowhere near complete. The final year was quite difficult because people had to move on with their careers, not opening up new things to do but finishing old things as best they could. So it was a rather strange time. We were going through the death throes. It was very sad.

Lesley Moore

It makes you want to scream

That last staff meeting in Saxon Court in March 1992 – the end of the Milton Keynes Development Corporation – was absolutely awesome. A whole load of grown men just crying. It was incredible, unbelievable. People you would never have expected to be emotionally affected by it. After '92, they stopped new-town development corporations and now they're talking about Milton Keynes expanding again and they might bring a special purpose vehicle back, which might be like a development corporation. It makes you want to scream. We've lost ten years.

Anon

Who's running the show?

The new phase of development is not being tied into the whole ethos of the city. With the potential for lots more expansion, I just wonder who's running the show?

Debbie Greaves

Changes are the problem

The Master Plan is the thing that makes Milton Keynes successful. It's the changes to the Master Plan that have caused the problems.

David Stabler

The beauty was the balance

The Corporation had very set rules, like there wouldn't be a building over three storeys high. I'm just a bit worried that that vision has tarnished and it's becoming overcrowded and

The Living Archive Band at the annual music festival, Folk on the Green, Stony Stratford, 1994.

overbuilt and the space is going. I think the beauty was the balance between putting in a lot of houses and people, but keeping a country feel as well.

Janice Walker

Cracks might appear

Before Milton Keynes moves on to the next phase, I'd like to see consolidation, at least for a while, and consider how big we want to get. Personally, I wouldn't like to see this become a metropolis. If it gets too big, too quick, then cracks might appear. I wouldn't like to see this fabulous town, which I feel part of, which I intend to stay in, be damaged.

Tracy Walters

We can make a difference

It's been the most amazing thirty years of endless job opportunity. Lots of people have been able to shape their own destiny. A testimony to the place is that my kids, who I thought would run a mile from it, have actually come back and lived here. The good thing about Milton Keynes is that most people have chosen to come here. It's open, it's pioneering – it's been that kind of place. That's why we're fiercely patriotic about the place. And we can make a difference.

Roger Kitchen